Praise for

THE
SELLING of
the AMERICAN
ECONOMY

THE SELLING of the AMERICAN ECONOMY

HOW FOREIGN COMPANIES ARE REMAKING THE AMERICAN DREAM

MICHELINE MAYNARD

BROADWAY BOOKS

NEW YORK

Library of Congress Cataloging-in-Publication Data
Maynard, Micheline.
    The selling of the American economy: how foreign companies are remaking
the American dream / Micheline Maynard. — 1st ed.
        p.   cm.
    Includes bibliographical references and index.
    1. International business enterprises—United States. 2. United States—
Economic conditions—2001– I. Title.
    HD2753.U5M39 2009
    338.8'8873—dc22   2009023325

ISBN 978-0-385-52052-2

Printed in the United States of America

10 9 8 7 6 5 4 3 2 1

First Edition

To the American worker

Contents

Introduction 1

Chapter One | The Selling of the American Economy 15

Chapter Two | The Invisible Worker 45

Chapter Three | Foreign Capital 65

Chapter Four | Not in My Backyard 85

Chapter Five | Not in Washington's Backyard, Either 105

Chapter Six | Foreign Owners, American Management 129

Chapter Seven | The Welcome Mat 159

Chapter Eight | The Race Between the States 183

Chapter Nine | A View from the Top 201

Chapter Ten | The New Face of the American Economy 227

Acknowledgments 249

References 251

Index 255

THE
SELLING of
the AMERICAN
ECONOMY

Introduction

It comes as no surprise upon meeting Amy Lindsey to learn that she once worked for Estée Lauder, the giant cosmetics company known for brands such as Clinique, MAC, and Bobbi Brown that are worn by millions of women all over the world. Five foot three, perky, with brown hair and blond highlights, she arrived for the interview wearing blue eyeliner that coordinated nicely with her stylish outfit, blue earrings, and matching necklace. Although her management position with the cosmetics company fit with her sense of fashion, Lindsey, then a single mother of a grade-school daughter, left in search of a new position with more regular hours, a better salary, and the opportunity for advancement.

She found it in Princeton, Indiana, at the Toyota plant.

Friends thought she was kidding when Lindsey, a graduate of Eastern Illinois University with a degree in speech communications, first applied for her position at the factory where Toyota makes the Sienna minivan and the Highlander, a crossover vehicle like an SUV. Hardly a car buff, with no experience in manufacturing or engineering, Lindsey spends much of her day behind the wheel of a delivery cart, bringing bins of parts to the assembly line. "We can see it now," her best friend joked, "the lipstick hard hat on a fork truck." That's exactly what she is, Lindsey said, unapologetically. "I'm not going to change who I am because I'm going to work in a factory."

One thing has changed, however. Instead of the cosmetician's smock she wore behind a counter selling Estée Lauder in Orlando, Florida, she now dons a uniform consisting of a blue shirt with her first name stitched on the chest next to the Toyota logo, protective covers over her sleeves, and khaki pants with steel-toed boots. It is quite literally blue-collar attire and nothing anyone else might see as glamorous, but she still considers herself a fashion plate. "Look at how cute the uniforms are," she said, standing up to provide a good look.

Lindsey, who grew up in Mount Carmel, Illinois, about twenty miles from the plant, considers herself lucky to have her job at Toyota, which allowed her to move back up north from Florida to be closer to her family. And she is not alone. Lindsey is one of more than five million Americans, or roughly 10 percent of the country's industrial workforce, employed by companies based overseas. At a time when American-owned companies are hemorrhaging jobs, closing plants, and slashing pensions and benefits, foreign companies have become a lifeline for workers like Lindsey and her colleagues.

Foreign companies often touch a nerve in American society and are still the objects of fear and distrust among many, who view foreign investment as a threat not just to the American worker but to the American way of life. But this xenophobic attitude couldn't be further from the truth. Because, in fact, foreign investment is not simply about allowing workers like Lindsey to pick up a weekly paycheck. Foreign companies that invest in our economy are having a significant—and largely positive—impact on not only the lives of workers but on the health of the American economy and society as a whole.

In today's flattened world, foreign companies are playing a larger and larger role not only in our national economy but in our states, towns, and communities—by hiring American workers where few other employment opportunities exist; pumping money into state, regional, and local economies; contributing money to schools, parks, and towns; and teaching Americans new ways to live and work. Investments by big car companies such as Toyota, Honda, Nissan, and Mercedes-Benz have received the greatest share of attention over the past few years, simply because their factories cost so much money to build—usually at least $1 billion apiece—and because each one provides one thousand jobs or more at a single location. In other words, those numbers talk, not to just the media and the political pundits but to state lawmakers, community leaders, governors, and mayors, and to workers who see a chance at a new future.

But the scope of foreign companies doing business in the United States is by no means confined to the auto industry. There are also tens of thousands of Americans working at such companies as India's Tata Group, which operates the Pierre Hotel in New York and makes Eight O'Clock Coffee; the European Aeronautic Defence and Space Company (EADS), the Franco-German aircraft consortium that builds helicopters in

3

Mississippi and is vying for a contract to build refueling planes for the U.S. Air Force in Alabama; and Haier, the Chinese appliance maker, with a refrigerator plant in South Carolina and an impressive headquarters housed in a landmark building in midtown Manhattan. Among dozens of others, there is also the Swiss food company Nestlé, which employs hundreds of American workers to make Nesquik and Coffee-Mate in Indiana, and InBev, the Belgian beverage maker, which now owns one of the most American of brand names, Anheuser-Busch.

While foreign companies often get the most attention for the number of workers they employ, the economic power they wield extends far beyond the jobs they directly create. When a foreign company opens a plant or factory, or buys a business in a region, it not only employs its own workers, it also stimulates local commerce and creates a demand for more homes, shops, schools, and restaurants. What's more, it lures companies from other sectors—suppliers, consultants, technicians, and so forth—who then provide countless more jobs by opening up satellite factories in the area. That is why these companies are so often courted by governors, mayors, and economic development officials eager to bring these benefits of this investment to their states and communities.

Lindsey recalled the excitement in her area in the mid-1990s when word came that Toyota would build a plant in southern Indiana, a short drive from Evansville and a few hours away from St. Louis, Missouri, and Louisville, Kentucky. "It just had a huge impact. People had the vision to know it was going to change communities," she said. For proof, local residents merely had to look three hours east to Georgetown, Kentucky, the home of Toyota's first freestanding car factory in the United States.

Once a hamlet that housed just a college and a few downtown cafés, Georgetown has tripled in size in the two decades since Toyota arrived, with new schools, roads, freeway exits, and dozens of expensive homes, many of which were built—either directly or indirectly—because of Toyota. Even Fort Branch, Indiana, where Lindsey's family lives, has seen the benefits conferred by her employer. In the past few years, it built two new parks through contributions from Toyota, while her daughter's grade school, Holy Cross, recently received six thousand dollars' worth of computers from the company.

Getting a job at a foreign company isn't always easy; standards are high, competition is fierce, and the hiring process can be arduous. For Lindsey, who is in her early forties, getting hired at Toyota was no simple matter. After being invited to come in for an initial job interview, she spent three eight-hour days on a simulated assembly line, taking part in a test meant to see whether she had the aptitude for repetitive work. Only then was she permitted to fill out a formal application for an assembly line position. When she did so, Lindsey specified the more-desirable first shift, which runs from dawn to early afternoon, so she could be home when her daughter, Ellie, returned from school.

That proved to be a mistake. There were far more qualified workers than there were positions available, and many got priority because they were willing to take shifts anytime during the day or night. Ultimately, Lindsey's application was rejected; to make matters worse, under Toyota's rules (adopted so that the company could work through thousands of applicants), Lindsey had to wait two years before she could apply again. The next time, she was better prepared. Before she submitted her new application, her family members promised that they could help look after Ellie in the hours she was not home, giving her the flexibility to tell Toyota she was willing to work either the day or night shift, thus increasing her chances.

Even after Toyota accepted her second application, it took another full year until she was hired. Eventually, however, a call came saying she had been chosen for a job at the plant. "It was very exciting—scary and exciting at the same time," she said. Lindsey went to work in May 2002, and in her first eleven months, she was assigned to the night shift, leaving little time available to spend with her daughter. It was a difficult adjustment. Many nights, she got home at 1 a.m. and was awake until 2:45 a.m., unable to unwind from her new routine. She also wasn't used to being active for such a long stretch, and after she started the job she found herself with sore muscles for weeks.

But this difficult period didn't last long, and for the past seven years, she has worked the daytime hours she originally requested. And because she was assigned to the minivan assembly line, Lindsey has worked steadily throughout the toughest time the automobile industry has seen in years, even remaining on the job when the plant's other assembly line was shut down in 2008 and early 2009 after the plant eliminated production of pickup trucks and shifted over to build the Highlander.

Her routine begins at dawn. Once she arrives at the plant, an imposing structure painted light gray and cream that sits back from a busy four-lane highway, she starts her day by reading through the plant newspaper, then performs a series of stretches to limber up for her job on the factory floor. Workers have learned to continue the exercises whenever they get the chance during the day, in order to reduce the stress on their legs, back, and arms. The exercises are surprisingly effective, Lindsey said. Now, the only strain she usually feels are "a few tweaks here and there."

Toyota officials had warned her of the physical nature of her new job before she joined the plant, but Lindsey, who stocked shelves during her time behind the Estée Lauder counter, was not daunted by such an active workday. She was more apprehensive that the position at a Japanese company might not sit well with her late father, Robert C. Fearheiley, a disabled veteran of World War II.

"I asked him, 'Are you okay with the fact that I would be working there?' " Lindsey said. Fearheiley answered, "I am so proud of you and so proud of the idea. I don't see GM and Ford coming down here and offering jobs."

This attitude toward foreign companies, while not shared by all, is gaining some traction in American society, thanks in part to efforts companies such as Toyota are making to ingratiate themselves with American consumers. Because of Lindsey's position, for example, her parents began driving a Toyota Avalon sedan (built at the plant in Kentucky), which they purchased under a Toyota program that offers a discount to employees' family members. But that was a modest perk compared with the real payoff from her Toyota job. "I make almost three times what I made" at Estée Lauder, she said, where she earned $31,000 a year after being promoted to counter manager, and where there were no retirement benefits, not even a 401(k) plan.

"Here, I have a pension fully funded by Toyota," she said,

not to mention a much higher salary, of about $65,000 a year, plus an annual bonus whose size depends on whether the plant achieves certain goals.

In addition to greater professional autonomy, a higher salary, and superior benefits, companies such as Toyota also offer their workers more job security than their American counterparts. This is partially a cultural thing—in Japan, where people tend to switch jobs far less often throughout their lifetimes than in America, employees feel more loyalty to their companies, and their companies are more loyal to them in return.

In 2008, for example, after a slump in big truck sales (caused by a spike in gas prices) forced Toyota to suspend production of pickup trucks at the Princeton plant and move pickup work to its plant in San Antonio, no full-time staff member was permanently laid off. Instead, during the time the pickup line was idle, workers were paid to conduct maintenance projects inside the factory, take part in job-training sessions, and come up with ways to improve the use of machinery on the assembly line. When it came time in 2009 for Toyota to consider cutting jobs, it still did not let any permanent workers go. Instead, it offered them voluntary buyouts that included ten weeks' pay, two weeks in additional pay for every year they had worked at the plant, and another $20,000 on top of that. There were few takers, however; in such an uncertain economy, workers were not anxious to give up jobs at a company whose future was not in doubt.

The preliminaries over, Lindsey sets off for a busy shift as a parts coordinator. Her tasks include sorting parts into yellow plastic bins, loading the bins onto carts used to deliver the parts to workers at their stations, driving the convoy to spots where the parts are needed on the assembly line, and unloading the bins onto racks. That might sound mundane, but her job involves more than just transporting parts. At Toyota, all employees, from the assembly line workers on up, are encouraged to play an active role in spotting and solving problems, and Lindsey said she is constantly watching the assembly line for signs that production has slowed or become interrupted. If she spots a slowdown, her first move is to find a team leader, easily identifiable by the stripe on his or her hard hat and the handheld radio that is always nearby. Should she see that workers are running low on parts but are too busy to request more, she has the authority to automatically add an extra bin or two to her next delivery. "I won't wait for them to call and say, 'Hey, we're down three parts, could somebody run some out?' " Lindsey said.

To some, a job in a factory delivering parts might sound like a step down for a college graduate, and might pale in comparison to a more glamorous job at a cosmetics company. The job has not been without its difficult moments, such as her sleepless nights and aches and pains. But to Lindsey, it's well worth it; her position at Toyota offers opportunities for personal growth and advancement she didn't have at Estée Lauder. In fact, it is something she can see doing for the rest of her working career. And she is certain that she will not spend another quarter century delivering plastic bins of parts on an assembly line. Looking around the factory, where employees have risen from jobs on the assembly line to senior management positions, she knows there will be plenty of opportunities for her to do other kinds of work along the way. "I will" retire from the plant, she says.

Lindsey is just one among millions of Americans working at factories, hotels, shops, engineering centers, and other businesses and facilities opened or owned by foreign companies in the United States. She and those like her provide a lens through which to look at an increasingly important and often overlooked part of the American economy and society.

Despite its powerful and far-reaching impact, the role of foreign investment in America has not been completely understood, until now. While much has been written about certain aspects of globalization—off-shoring, outsourcing, and sending American investment overseas—this book tells the unique, unexamined stories on the flip side of that coin. Of all the hundreds of companies that could have fit this bill, I've chosen to focus primarily on four major foreign players, Toyota, EADS, Tata, and Haier, for two specific reasons. First, they represent the major regions, industries, and business centers of the world. (Although Canada is the single biggest country that trades with the United States, few Canadian companies have equivalent stature worldwide.) Second, their various sizes, levels of visibility, and degrees of involvement in our society offer a complete and colorful portrait of foreign investment in the United States.

Without question, Toyota is one of the best-known foreign companies in the United States, and perhaps the world. But more than just a case study, Toyota is a symbol of the far-reaching impact a foreign company can have on a country. Toyota's actions represent those not only of its company but also of the globalization model itself, just as General Motors stood for unfettered capitalism a generation ago. As a journalist who has covered Toyota for much of her adult life, I know the Toyota story very well, and I believe that it speaks volumes about the nature and impact of foreign investment in America.

I chose EADS, the owner of Airbus, not only because it is one of Europe's most influential companies, with roots in its three most important economies, Britain, France, and Germany, but also because, since Airbus is the only challenger to Boeing in the global aviation field (EADS's other companies are key players in the global military equipment market), its American investments receive a huge amount of attention and generate considerable controversy. Through my work at the *New York Times*, I've watched EADS and Airbus become increasingly prominent in their fields. (It was an Airbus jet, after all, that was involved in the "Miracle on the Hudson," in which 150 passengers owed their lives to the smart thinking of Captain Chesley Sullenberger.) I was also privy to much of what has gone on behind the scenes as the company has struggled against the public and political resistance against its U.S. presence.

EADS has ambitions to become to aviation and military equipment what Toyota has become to the American automobile market: a rival doing business on its own turf. Unlike Toyota, however, it has not shied from debate, and it can expect even more in years to come. In taking on the American icon Boeing, EADS, to put it bluntly, has proved itself to be a gutsy company, with big ambitions. It is an organization that Americans should keep their eyes on.

Like EADS, Haier of China has also chosen a bold approach with its American investments. It makes an interesting case study, primarily because its very presence in the United States in the first place is so puzzling. Why would a Chinese company, with access to so much inexpensive labor, an economy that is expanding at an amazing rate, and the safety net of government backing, seek to make inroads in the American market? It would seem to be simpler just to stay home. Furthermore, in entering this market, Haier, unlike other foreign companies, did not send its own executives and managers to do the work. It chose to let Americans set up its operations, fostering an exchange of talents, ideas, and innovation that global companies rarely display at the outset of their investments. Through Haier, we can gain a better understanding of the potential of Chinese companies in the United States, which seems to have evaded the attention of most business journalists, who focus much of the discussion and debate on American companies doing business in China.

Lastly, Tata of India is worth studying because, despite the ubiquity of its many and varied products and holdings in the United States, it remains a mystery to many Americans. Yet its experience here is instructive, demonstrating the obstacles many foreign entities must surmount in order to be accepted by the American public. I first came across Tata's products when I visited the Geneva Motor Show several years ago on an assignment for *Fortune* magazine. I was intrigued by the idea of what Indian cars looked like and went out of my way to seek out their tiny display. The Tata associates on the scene seemed happy for the attention, and I still have the box of Tata Tea that I was given as a souvenir. Ever since then, I have followed the company in all its guises. Tata is ready for prime time.

I have also selected these particular examples because in order to understand the full impact of foreign investment on our economy and society, one must also understand how it is experienced and perceived. Too often, foreign companies are depicted as something to be feared. Some critics contend that welcoming—in some cases, courting—investments by companies such as Toyota, Tata, EADS, and Haier is somehow unpatriotic or even dangerous. To them, it amounts to selling our economy to the highest bidder. But if foreign investment is growing our economy, transforming our communities, enriching our culture, and making us more competitive in the global marketplace, then is "selling" pieces of the economy really such a bad thing?

That's a question I will raise in this book. I hope you will come away with a new understanding of how foreign investment is transforming the American Dream. At a time when the country is at a crossroads, and there is so much uncertainty about how we can recover from one of the most difficult periods of our history, the role of foreign investment in our economy and our society is simply too crucial to ignore.

Chapter One

THE
SELLING of
the AMERICAN
ECONOMY

Above and beyond the question of how to grow the economy, there is a legitimate concern about how to grow the quality of our lives.

—PAUL WELLSTONE

Americans would like to think of this country as the most self-sufficient place on earth, able to feed, clothe, employ, and educate its citizens—and those in need elsewhere—with no help from anyone else. To the most patriotic, there is no country on a par in any way with the United States, no matter the economic traumas it may encounter. "I do believe in American Exceptionalism," Senator John McCain said in September 2008, even as our credit system had collapsed, some of our biggest investment banks had fallen, and unemployment had reached a new high. If there was ever a time foreign investment was needed, it is now. Today, when the business world has lost its borders and companies are no longer bound by the nations in which they were founded, no one nation—no matter how exceptional—can sustain itself through homegrown investment alone.

In our increasingly interconnected world, one thing has

become strikingly clear. Foreign investment is a necessary and positive force in the American economy, as long as those companies act responsibly, give back to American communities, and provide Americans with stable jobs for which they are fairly compensated. At a time when American companies have closed plants, laid off millions of workers, and ventured abroad in search of profits, foreign companies offer an attractive alternative—in some cases, the only one.

Many believe that foreign investment in the United States is a relatively new phenomenon, one that gained attention on the national stage as recently as the 1980s, when Japanese automakers opened their first American factories and when other Japanese investors went on a real estate buying spree. But in reality, foreign investment is older than our nation itself, dating back to the 1600s, when English and Dutch traders crossed the Atlantic seeking opportunities on our shores. In fact, the Jamestown colony, the first colony formed in the New World, was founded by British entrepreneurs from the Virginia Company. They manufactured soap, pitch, glass, and wood building supplies—some of the very first American-made products to be exported to Europe.

From the beginning of the republic until well into the late 1800s, much of the foreign investment that took place in the United States was from Britain, which is no surprise, since, of course, this nation began as a series of British colonies. But other countries—France, Germany, and Spain among them—soon sought their own investments in the United States, in some cases helping to create entire industries. During the Civil War, after President Lincoln ordered the blockade of Southern ports, crafty British blockade runners, operating in small, fast ships, helped sustain the economy in the South by bringing in goods from Bermuda, the Bahamas, and Cuba, sending illegal shipments of cotton and tobacco there in return. In *Gone with the Wind*, Rhett Butler made his fortune doing business with these foreign traders, earning the enmity of the proper citizens of Atlanta.

In more modern terms, foreign companies have been investing in America in earnest since the nineteenth century, when companies such as England's Lever soap company, the forerunner of the Anglo-Dutch Unilever subsidiary Lever Brothers, opened plants in Massachusetts and Mississippi. We can attribute a good portion of our nation's early infrastructure to foreign dollars; in the 1870s, foreign investors, particularly Dutch capitalists, bankrolled the expansion of the nation's railroad system. In fact, foreign players had a hand in just about every corner of our industrial economy during the nineteenth century, buying stakes in everything from the Pennsylvania steel mills to the copper mines in northern Michigan to the gold mines of Alaska and the West.

By the early 1900s, as the nation's immigrant population boomed, foreign investment became as integral to the U.S. economy as the coal and oil powering the plants and factories; while most new arrivals were poor, a number of deep-pocketed immigrants such as John Jacob Astor and Andrew Carnegie quickly joined the ranks of the most influential business tycoons of the era.

But Americans' reaction to foreign investment has always peaked and crested with political sentiment, and after 1914, the welcome mat was yanked away from the door. Once World War I broke out, German companies became, almost overnight, a target for angry Americans, who linked their presence here to the hostilities raging in Europe. Some German investors were accused of spying, and many even saw their American assets taken over by the government—an inherent risk for any company that invests abroad at a time of political conflict. It wasn't until the boom times of the 1920s, when the specter of the war had receded and investments from around the world flooded into Wall Street, that foreign investment resumed its prominent role in the American economy.

The flood of foreign money continued throughout the 1930s and '40s, as English, German, and Japanese auto companies began to build factories across the United States. Japanese factories in the United States are widely thought to be a product of the 1970s, but, in reality, Japanese and other Asian companies had begun to build plants in the United States before World War II, just as Detroit automobile companies had already begun to build factories in Japan—GM in Osaka, and Ford in Yokohama. After WWII, of course, this flood of capital came to a screeching, if temporary, halt, as our defeated opponents were forced to focus on rebuilding their own economies from the ravages of the war. Once they recovered, however, old grudges were forgotten, and investment, particularly from Asia, soon resumed, picking up in the 1970s when a confluence of events in the United States—the oil crisis and subsequent rise in demand for smaller, more fuel-efficient vehicles, as well as new protectionist policies limiting Japanese imports—compelled Japanese automakers and other producers to shift production to our shores.

During the past quarter century, foreign investment has become increasingly more prominent and more powerful in our economy and society, as countless companies from abroad have taken on the roles that once belonged only to homegrown players: creating American jobs, helping bolster American school systems, rescuing struggling companies, reviving stagnating towns, transforming states, and restoring vigor to entire regions of the country. The critical involvement of global companies and economies in our own has never been so evident as when the financial crisis shook the country in 2008.

Despite a $700 billion congressional bailout and drastic measures by the Treasury Department and the Federal Reserve, after the banking system collapsed that September, it became almost immediately clear that America could not solve its problems alone. It took a coalition of global efforts to stem the market crash that threatened not only the American economy but also banks and businesses abroad, as European countries, Japan, China, and other nations were forced to step in with their own rescue plans, hoping to ease a crisis that could take years to resolve.

Yet, despite the many benefits of a global economy—brought into even sharper focus during times of turmoil—foreign investment in the United States is often a trigger for resentment, fear, or, at the least, ambiguity about the role that outsiders should play. This is not a feeling held singularly by Americans, of course. The populaces of other nations, including Britain, have found themselves reeling when foreign companies purchased their icons, and protectionist sentiment continues to resound worldwide as companies from growing economic powers such as China, India, and Russia begin to expand farther and farther beyond their borders. But in spite of the visceral reaction so many of us have when foreign companies break ground or buy up companies on our shores, the fact remains that the global economy envelops us all.

To be sure, the presence of foreign investors in the United States today is formidable. Foreign direct investment, defined as spending by a foreign-owned company on company-owned ventures or investments in American enterprises, comprises 15 percent of the gross domestic product (GDP), according to the Treasury Department. More than 5.3 million workers are employed by foreign companies in the United States, akin to five companies the size of Walmart. What's more, those jobs have led to 4.6 million jobs in other parts of the economy, for a total of nearly 10 million people who owe their livelihoods to companies based abroad.

Think of it this way: If all those jobs disappeared and the people who hold them were not able to find work, the unemployment rate in the United States would stand at more than 13 percent, instead of more than 9 percent in 2009. The loss of jobs on such a scale would be a huge blow, sending ripple effects across the economy. Not only that, but the economy simply cannot sustain itself in the absence of foreign investment. Over the past twenty years, foreign companies have invested more than $2 trillion in the American economy, according to a report by Matthew Slaughter, a professor and associate dean at the Tuck School of Business at Dartmouth. In 2007 alone, those companies opened or expanded nearly 760 American factories, creating 52,000 new American jobs and $35.5 billion in capital spending. "The establishment and expansion of foreign companies in the United States has forced people to think harder about who we are economically," Professor Slaughter said.

JOBS ARE JOBS

In researching this book, I asked countless public officials, economists, and executives why investment from overseas is such a necessary part of the American economy. Each time, I received the exact same answer: jobs. Samuel Adcock, the senior vice president of government affairs for EADS, said, "You can argue about the name above the door . . . [but] at some point, new American jobs are American jobs."

This very sentiment—that jobs are jobs—is how Michigan's governor, Jennifer M. Granholm, firmly defended the half dozen foreign trade missions she has made since taking office in 2003, all aimed at bringing investments in research and technology to her beleaguered state. "I'll go anywhere and do anything to bring jobs to Michigan," she told me, even as she fervently pleaded in Washington for a bailout for her state's carmakers. Donald Grimes, an economist with the Institute for Labor and Industrial Relations at the University of Michigan, one of the country's top economic forecasters, completely endorses this line of reasoning. Grimes, who is well known to listeners of National Public Radio and viewers of *The NewsHour with Jim Lehrer* on PBS, regularly compiles data that is used by the governors and legislatures of a number of states, including Michigan. Resistance to foreign investment "goes against the fundamental idea that the world is a more integrated place" he said. "Look at these jobs—there are *lots* of jobs here."

Those jobs are everywhere—not just in traditional manufacturing centers such as Detroit or the Rust Belt. Foreign companies employ Americans everywhere from Alaska to Florida; there are foreign-owned companies employing American workers in every one of the fifty states. In Indiana alone, for example, one out of every seven manufacturing jobs comes from a company based outside the United States. And the payoff has been invaluable. Without foreign investment, said Mitch Daniels, the Republican governor of Indiana, "We'd be a dust bowl."

Foreign investment has been the single most important economic factor that has helped lift the Deep South out of the past and into a high-tech future. It is a collective strategy that could be seen as the South's economic revenge on the North, some 150 years after the end of the Civil War. Governors from South Carolina to Texas, from Kentucky to Georgia have relentlessly courted foreign companies, using the lures of tax breaks, laws that make it difficult for unions to organize, and their courtly hospitality. In short, they want foreign investment and will do whatever it takes to get it.

With good reason: Few states have reaped the benefits of foreign investment more than Mississippi, Alabama, and Tennessee, often referred to as "Detroit South" because of the influx of automotive plants in the past decade. (The political and economic power of these "new domestics" became evident in 2008, when southern lawmakers nicknamed "the Toyota Republicans" fought hard against the congressional bailout of the American automakers.) Nor are they finished. In the next decade, these states hope to join forces to create a development corridor for aviation, both commercial and military.

Even states that might seem to be bastions of American investment have healthy numbers of foreign-company employees, including nearly 200,000 workers in Michigan, long dominated by the American automobile industry. In Pennsylvania, where steel mills and coal mines have been traditional sources of blue-collar work, firms from outside the United States employ some 250,000 workers—some of them in mills now owned by foreign companies.

It is no surprise that California, which has long led the nation in embracing new trends and attracting immigration, has by far the most employees from foreign companies; more than 560,000 Californians earn a paycheck from a firm based outside the United States, according to the Organization for International Investment (OFII). Most of the Japanese auto companies, as well as Hyundai of Korea, have their American headquarters in California. The entertainment industry has a variety of companies such as Sony and Universal Studios (both, of course, based in California) that have a number of influential foreign shareholders. New York, with nearly 400,000 employees of foreign companies among its residents, is second in terms of the number of jobs created by foreign investment, largely because of investments in the financial sector. All told, this global payroll in the United States is more than $365 billion—about twice the GDP of Saudi Arabia. While the assembly line and unskilled jobs generally capture more attention, the fact is that these facilities also create large numbers of higher-paying managerial and skilled jobs, which are equally, if not more, important to a state's economic base.

Though in some parts of the country, the stigma of working for a foreign-owned company might still linger, Gary N. Chaison, professor of industrial relations at Clark University in Worcester, Massachusetts, theorizes it is largely gone. Tied to the stigma of buying foreign-made products, it started to disappear, he argues, when Americans started to buy Japanese products (mostly cameras and television sets) during the 1970s, and was further diluted once Americans started flocking to Japanese cars (which now comprise more than 40 percent of American automobile sales). Today, he reasons, with the recent flood of goods from China and other parts of Asia, the shame of buying from—or working for—an overseas company is largely gone. "The line is so blurred that there is no antipathy to working in the United States for a foreign firm," he says.

Many of the workers I spoke with feel the same way. Marty Chapman, the president of the chamber of commerce in Putnam County, West Virginia, said there was little concern among local residents about the implications of working for a foreign carmaker when Toyota opened an engine plant there in 1997. "They just wanted the jobs," he said. It is easy to understand why. Nearly one in four American manufacturing jobs has vanished since 2000, and forty thousand factories have closed since 1998, according to the Alliance for American Manufacturing, a Washington trade group. In 2008, in fact, as the economy crumbled and factory orders—everything from computer chips to steel casings—plummeted to record lows, manufacturing jobs accounted for nearly a third of all those lost in the United States. "We're at a point where a good job is a good job, and benefits are benefits, whether the companies are based here or somewhere else," said Chaison.

INVESTING IN AMERICA

Foreign investment has long been a lifeline not just to American workers but also to ailing American companies, making it a powerful force in the economy as a whole. America is the destination for more foreign investment than any other nation in the world, even China, despite the rush there during the recent years of its economic boom. While detractors say the profits from those companies only go back to places like Tokyo, Beijing, or Stuttgart, in reality, foreign companies reinvest 46 percent of the profits they earn in the United States in their American facilities, according to the Treasury Department.

At a time when many American companies cannot—or choose not to—invest in operations at home, foreign investment has become a critical, and necessary, source of capital. In 2007, foreign companies paid $42.4 billion in taxes to federal, state, and local governments, and spent even more—$43 billion—on research and development in the United States.

Among all the companies that have invested in the United States, one company has made an enormous impact on both our economy and our way of life: Toyota. In the past two decades, it has become a formidable example of what foreign investment can bring to the country. Since it opened its first American factory in Georgetown, Kentucky, in 1988, Toyota has invested nearly $20 billion in its facilities in the United States, Canada, and Mexico—or roughly $1 billion a year. It has created more than eighty thousand manufacturing-related jobs, and if the employees at its offices and its dealers are factored in, Toyota employs a quarter of a million people in North America.

But Toyota's role in our economy reaches even beyond the money it has generated and the jobs it creates. Toyota has opened dealerships, built parks, donated to school systems, kept arts organizations afloat, and put its own stamp on a collection of communities from coast to coast. Since 1998, it has also donated $400 million to cities and states where its factories, research centers, and offices are located; for example, when Toyota opened one of its newest facilities, in York Township, Michigan, in October 2008, the ceremony included the presentation of four checks for $25,000 to two area school systems, the state's economic development foundation, and to the township to maintain a 7.8-acre park that the company had previously donated. Toyota's philanthropy approached $60 million in 2008 alone, fulfilling the charitable role that Detroit companies once played in their heyday. Even though Toyota lost $3.9 billion in 2008 and expected a bigger loss in 2009, executives vowed the company still saw opportunities in the United States and would continue to invest.

When companies such as Toyota invest in a community, they not only create countless jobs and pump money into the local economy, they also stimulate local commerce and create demands that attract even more businesses to the region. By employing staffs of American-trained, American-born engineers, designers, and manufacturing experts, foreign companies can boost a state's profile—and its desirability to other companies and investors, both domestic and foreign, who flock to the region hoping to capitalize on this top talent and expertise.

EMOTIONAL VERSUS RATIONAL

The battle that foreign companies face in the United States is not just one for economic power; it is a highly emotional battle as well. Time and again, foreign companies have learned that their presence can trigger a visceral reaction among the American public that is less about the specific country they are from and more about the simple fact that they are not American. For many companies, this economic xenophobia, be it spoken or unspoken, can be nearly impossible to escape.

Toyota, for example, has navigated this treacherous ground for much of the past half century, ever since it began to operate in the United States. EADS, the European maker of airplanes and defense equipment (and a much newer entrant to the U.S. marketplace) has felt the brunt of protectionist sentiment during the past few years, especially after challenging Boeing, an American icon, for a $35 billion tanker contract from the air force. Haier, the Chinese appliance giant, felt the sting of political backlash when it tried to buy another well-known American brand, Maytag (eventually losing out to Whirlpool, which subsequently closed most of the Maytag factories that it so vigorously competed to buy). And more than a few eyebrows went up when Tata of India, the maker of the $2,500 mini car called the Nano, became the winning bidder for the luxury brands owned by the Ford Motor Company.

This battle for hearts and minds poses a number of serious challenges for foreign companies, ones that can't be underestimated or ignored. But why does it matter so much to Americans whether jobs are homespun or provided by firms from abroad? Why does foreign investment seem to touch such a populist nerve, even in states that stand to gain? If, as so many people I spoke with suggest, a job is just a job, why is it just so personal? Executives from Europe, Asia, and elsewhere, perplexed by some Americans' reaction, have been asking those questions for decades.

One answer is fear: fear of what is unknown, fear of what is different, fear that if foreign companies are allowed to compete with American ones, they will win, putting venerable American institutions out of business. But the reality is that foreign competition is actually quite healthy; it drives down consumer prices and fosters innovation, bringing new products to market and making us *more* competitive on a global scale, not less.

Another answer is that in a society that so values individual achievement, our companies speak to the world about us. This fundamental, if flawed, American belief, what scholar Howard Zinn has described as the Myth of American Exceptionalism— the notion that America is the divine homeland of liberty and economic opportunity, with everything to teach the world and nothing to learn from it. This concept still perpetuates much of American culture (or, at least, the dwindling part of our culture that has been untouched by influences from overseas). In this view, it is absolutely fine for GM to build cars in Spain or for Delta Air Lines to fly to every point on the globe; that is simply proof of American dominance. But for the reverse to happen somehow shakes our sense of self-worth. Of course, the thinking that we can or even should be the biggest and the best in any sector—autos, steel, retailing, military equipment—without any help from anyone seems counterintuitive in a global economy, and, often times, naïve.

After all, if American companies want to prosper, want to create innovative, high-quality products and services that compete in a global marketplace, they must be open to investment— not just in terms of dollars but in terms of technologies and ideas—outside the United States. The fact is that today, very few major companies, American, European, Asian, or otherwise, can be considered true global players if they compete only within their own borders. "It's amazing, on one level, that people even talk about companies as being national entities," said Donald Grimes.

So, why is it all right in the eyes of some Americans for firms from the United States to invest elsewhere (as long, of course, as that investment doesn't result in a loss of American jobs or capital), but not acceptable for a Japanese or a Korean or a German company to purchase an American company or open a new factory on our shores? After all, most Americans, Grimes said, would chafe at the idea if they were suddenly told that they could not buy stock in foreign companies traded on Wall Street, or mutual funds that invest in international companies. So why do we think we can spread our influence throughout the world while simultaneously closing our doors to others? Does it stem from a sense of nationalism or entitlement?

America is the country that goes out and invades other nations, whether through military or economic might. So why is it that foreign companies are often seen as the invaders—invaders of the modern-day American economy, which was supposed to be a place where Americans could thrive? Because, as some see it, foreign companies, instead of American ones, now have the money and the economic power and political clout that goes along with it. To them, this signals our failure to maintain our global status, to maintain the exceptionalism that has long been a source of national pride.

This short-sightedness misses the point that overall, foreign investment in the United States is not a sign of weakness; it is an endorsement that America remains a desirable—in fact, essential—place to do business for any company that wants to compete in a global economy. It also misses the point that foreign companies can be good for the American economy, if they act responsibly, invest in their communities, and most important, create stable jobs for American workers. In other words, it misses the point that we're not just the sellers in this equation, we're actually the buyers—buyers of a brighter economic future and, for millions of downtrodden American workers, buyers of the chance at a better life.

THE INVISIBLE WORKERS

No one can make this case better than the American workers themselves. All over the country, millions of Americans employed by foreign companies are buying homes, educating their children, and contributing as much or more to the economic base of their communities than employees of American companies. On average, they take home about $66,000 a year, according to the Treasury Department, or 20 percent more than their American-employed counterparts. And yet, these workers remain on the periphery of the American consciousness.

One reason for this is that unlike their counterparts at American companies, who are represented by prominent and vocal groups such as the United Steelworkers, the United Auto Workers, or the International Association of Machinists and Aerospace Workers, most of the workers employed by foreign companies are not unionized and have no collective identity, or voice, outside that of their companies.

Many companies from outside the United States have opted to put their operations in the twenty-two Right to Work states across the country, where workers cannot be compelled to join unions, even if their factory or office decides to organize. One reason is simply to save money; nonunion workers typically demand lower wages compared with the rates the foreign companies pay back home. The other is to foster an environment of open communication between workers and their employers, rather than having to constantly deal with intermediaries. Yet this rightfully raises a fear that since workers have no union to speak for them, the only voice they have is their own, and in the din that surrounds the American debate over foreign investments, their voices, and indeed their very existence, is often overlooked or forgotten.

But all of the foreign companies know that even if workers can't be forced to unionize, if they push their workers too hard or if they do not provide stable employment, or if conditions inside their factories are grim, workers will turn to the one option that lies before them: joining a union. Although the American labor movement is not as powerful as it was twenty to thirty years ago when a quarter of American workers were union members, and although many union drives have failed at auto and other plants in the past few decades, joining a union still remains a possibility. That knowledge constantly weighs on these companies and in most cases is enough to ensure fair treatment of their employees.

A TWO-WAY LIFELINE: THE STATES

Foreign investment can be a lifeline in a time of economic crisis, a sought-after substitute as American companies, declaring America to be too expensive a place to do business, have shut factories and put the bulk of their investments in plants overseas. This is why so many governors, state officials, and community leaders across the United States are eager to offer millions of dollars in incentives, such as new roads, training centers, and even land for factories and office buildings, to lure overseas companies to their regions.

One can hardly blame them. As soon as a foreign-owned factory announces plans to open in a new town, tens of thousands of workers often flock to apply for the few hundred newly created positions. This, in turn, stimulates local commerce, packing shops and restaurants and creating demand for more housing, schools, parks, and public works projects. In the case of large factories, dozens of parts suppliers and other supporting businesses, some from the countries where the main plant is based, open satellite factories that provide thousands of more jobs and bring more economic diversity to the region. This is why officials in Mississippi greeted Toyota with all the southern hospitality they could muster—not to mention $294 million in incentives—when Toyota announced plans in 2007 to open a plant there. (The plan has now been delayed by the economic downturn.)

Just ask the residents of Buffalo, West Virginia, former population 144, which was just a drive-through spot outside of Charleston—blink and you'd miss it—before Toyota opened its engine plant there in 1997. Today, it's been transformed into a thriving area, with jobs for more than 1,400 former teachers, telemarketers, and delivery company managers who come to work every day from twenty-seven out of West Virginia's fifty-five counties. Such investments "can literally put a town on the map," said John Casesa, a veteran investment analyst with the Casesa Shapiro Group in New York.

To be sure, some community groups are alarmed when a foreign company is rumored to be considering a local investment. Objections from local environmentalists—who feared a new factory would mean more pollution, both from the factory emissions itself and from idling engines on congested local roads—and from longtime citizens who simply resisted any disruption to the community, were reasons Toyota took a site in western Virginia off its list a few years ago when it was choosing a location for its eighth North American assembly plant. And, as we will see, labor groups in old union-dominated towns like Detroit are often vocal in their opposition to foreign investment. Yet many eventually come to realize what a boon foreign investment can be to their towns and communities.

A TWO-WAY LIFELINE: THE COMPANIES

It would be misleading to depict foreign investors simply as white knights, swooping in heroically to save an ailing American economy in distress. In reality, the benefits of foreign investment go both ways—as one would expect in a free-market society.

Despite the growth of emerging markets, such as China, India, and Russia, the United States remains the world's biggest and potentially most lucrative consumer goods market, one in which foreign companies need to operate in order to prosper on a global basis. This is why steel companies such as Severstal of Russia and ArcelorMittal of Luxembourg have purchased American mills, why InBev, the huge Belgian beer maker, purchased Anheuser-Busch in 2008, and why Fiat, a company that had been absent from the American market since 1994, agreed to take up to 35 percent of Chrysler in January 2009.

Consumer goods companies are not the only ones that can pour money into the United States. Investments by banks based overseas have become an increasingly critical source of capital in the wake of the 2008 banking crisis; for example, Britain's Barclays Capital bought up Lehman Brothers' investment arm after the company went bankrupt, and Hong Kong's HSBC put aside $3.2 billion to cover bad loans in the U.S. market in 2008. Sovereign wealth funds, the state-owned investment tools operated by nations as diverse as Abu Dhabi, Norway, Russia, and Singapore, have become active investors in our economy as well, taking stakes in private equity holders such as New York's Blackstone Group and in Morgan Stanley, one of the last remaining American investment banks. (These funds are just one type of international investment—others include international reserves, public pension funds, and state-owned enterprises—but they have received the most attention because of their size.) Thanks in part to their U.S. holdings, these funds, estimated in 2008 to hold $2.7 trillion, could grow to contain as much as $17.5 trillion over the next few years, according an estimate by Merrill Lynch (before its acquisition by Bank of America in 2008). Even individual investors can make huge contributions to an American company, such as the Mexican billionaire Carlos Slim Helú, who owns 6.9 percent of the media giant (and my employer) the New York Times Company.

But the reciprocal relationship between U.S. companies and their foreign investors is about more than just jobs, profits, and market share. The two-way exchange of ideas, skills, technology, and management methods are almost as valuable as the investments themselves. For Americans, working for a foreign company can provide an invaluable education, just as there is a great deal foreign executives can learn from their American counterparts.

THE POLITICAL IMPACT

While foreign investors have gained support through the years among governors and lawmakers, Democrat and Republican alike, the debate over foreign investment rages on. The situation has created some strange bedfellows, from Michigan's veteran Democratic congressman John Dingell to Mississippi Republican senator Trent Lott. It has also led to some uncomfortable moments and stirred up a fair amount of political controversy. One example was the firestorm of protest in the midst of the 2008 presidential primary campaign over the air force's decision to award a $35 billion contract to a collective of companies that included the European-controlled EADS, rather than to Boeing of Washington State.

Many foreign companies have learned (as EADS did, the hard way) that if they want to do business in the United States, they must integrate themselves not only into the fabric of states and communities but into the national political fray, as well. To this end, foreign companies spend hundreds of millions of dollars on lobbying, take part in industry trade groups, and bring experienced political hands onto their staffs for help. Samuel Adcock, EADS's chief lobbyist, for example, was the legislative director for Mississippi's Senator Lott, and Toyota's vice president of government affairs, Jo Cooper, was the executive director of the Alliance of American Automobile Manufacturers before she joined the Japanese automaker. Toyota's advisers also have included Sandy Berger, who was President Clinton's national security adviser and an international trade attorney. These companies, and dozens others, are members of the OFII, the primary trade group for foreign companies in the United

States. For as we will see, foreign companies have learned that they need to play the Washington game in order to gain widespread acceptance and make their voices heard.

FOUR MODELS OF FOREIGN INVESTMENT

Given the controversy that so often surrounds foreign investment, it's no surprise that, like any visitor from abroad who does not know local customs, styles, or even the language, foreign investors are often careful about their first steps in the United States. For some companies, protectionist threats and fear of calling attention to rookie mistakes are reasons enough to initially keep a low profile, while they establish their operations. For others, the United States is a place to "go big, or go home," so they try to integrate themselves into the fabric of our society in every possible way. But whatever their style or approach toward American investment may be, what all these companies have in common is that either in just a few years or over decades, they want to be powerful players in the American marketplace.

There are four primary ways that foreign companies approach their American investments, and they often have a lot to do with the degree to which a company integrates itself into American society. One method is simply to invest in an existing American company, by taking an ownership stake, forming a joint venture, or, in some cases, buying the company outright. This is the easiest way to enter the market, and in the case of ownership stakes and joint ventures, the least controversial. Retailers, banks, airlines, and food industry businesses often follow this path; some make a few choice acquisitions, some open a satellite branch or office in a U.S. city, and some buy up equity, as the German airline Lufthansa did in JetBlue, the low-fare airline based in Queens, New York, or as Fiat, the Italian carmaker, did in 2009, when it partnered with the Treasury to rescue Chrysler (Fiat agreed to oversee Chrysler's assets after it filed for bankruptcy, returning the company to foreign control after only eighteen months of American ownership). Stakes can often lead to joint venture arrangements, like the car-building deals during the 1980s between Toyota and GM, Ford and Mazda, and Chrysler and Mitsubishi. (Only the Toyota/GM deal survives, and neither company took a stake in the other.)

This is a method favored primarily by global brands with little wish to change an already honed identity, so these companies often abstain from participating in local civic or political affairs, except when necessary for regulatory or legal maters. Taking a stake is often an easier way to learn the ins and outs of the American market than purchasing a company outright, although that can happen, laws allowing, once a foreign firm understands how the American game is played. Rather than become a part of the American fabric, these firms are primarily another choice on a computer screen or a supermarket shelf, and their American holdings are merely a strategic inroad to the U.S. market and a way of gaining access to U.S. distribution channels.

A second strategy is to devise a plan for long-term growth but take things step by step. These cautious foreign firms may start by buying a single hotel or factory, figuring out the lay of the land, and then making more acquisitions and launching new ventures as they grow more comfortable operating in the American market. That is the strategy that Bertelsmann, the German media conglomerate, took when it entered the American publishing market during the 1980s. It began with smaller acquisitions, such as Bantam Books, which it purchased in 1980, and Doubleday, which it bought in 1986. By 1998, under a new chief executive, Thomas Middelhoff, it was ready to make a bold move, and it took over Random House, which became the umbrella for the media empire's worldwide book publishing operations. Tata of India, the giant holding group headed by Ratan Tata, has also followed this formula. Starting with a quiet series of investments, Tata has slowly built up more than twenty different businesses in the United States, where it is best known for hotels, food products, automobile development, and Internet consulting.

The third strategy is to leap into the American market with a big splash. Sometimes, this requires help from an American partner, as when EADS joined forces with Northrop Grumman to aggressively pursue a $35 billion contract to build tanker planes for the U.S. Air Force in Alabama. EADS, founded in 2000 through the merger of a series of European firms, had a modest foundation, with operations in Texas, Mississippi, and other states, some of which were acquired from other companies. But it saw the tanker contract as the catalyst for American expansion and a way to jump-start its efforts for further investment in the United States.

It has faced stiff opposition from Boeing in a battle (which we'll look at in more detail in chapter 4) that has grown bitter. In 2008, after initially awarding the contract to EADS, the air force decided to revisit the decision and begin the bidding process anew, a task that will now stretch for several more years. One compromise was floated in 2009 that would divide the big contract between the two companies, allowing both to create American jobs. But even if its bet on the tanker contract does not pay off, EADS has captured attention—for better or for worse—that other companies might take years to attract.

A fourth strategy is the most complex and risky for a foreign company: attempting to integrate itself so fully into our culture and our communities that it becomes akin to an American company. This is the path that Toyota has followed, one that has been the subject of both praise and criticism. Toyota's auto sales in the United States have now surpassed those at home in Japan, and its operations in the United States cover a wide swath of territory, from Michigan to Texas, and California to Washington, D.C. If its dealerships are included, Toyota can claim to employ Americans in every state. In fact, to some consumers, the Kentucky-built Toyota Camry and the Toyota Tundra pickup produced in Texas (where signs outside its San Antonio factory read "built in Texas, by Texans") seem almost as American as a Mercury sedan or a Ford SUV.

Toyota has become an "Americanized" company in part because it has treated the United States not only as a place to sell its vehicles but also as a country where it can both teach and learn new business practices that it can then apply around the world. In fact, its chairman, Fujio Cho, and Akio Toyoda, the grandson of the company's founder who was named its president in 2009, trained in the United States before rising within the company.

But embracing American business practices and hiring American workers is not enough to ensure American success. To be truly secure in their American presence, Toyota, Tata, Haier, EADS, and other foreign companies that make major investments here have learned they must win American hearts and minds, both in order to sell their products and to generate support that can be used to fend off their critics.

THE REALITY OF A GLOBAL MARKET

Of course, in today's complex and volatile global marketplace, foreign investment is no magical solution in and of itself. Foreign-owned ventures here are not always successful; after all, companies are only as smart as the people who run them, and plenty of foreign companies have suffered as a result of the mistakes their executives have made in the American market. There is certainly no guarantee that a job at a foreign company will be any more secure than a job at an American one in recent years; companies ranging from Volkswagen to Nestlé and Electrolux to Nokia have all had to shut down American factories and shift jobs elsewhere (though two of them, VW and Nestlé, returned afterward).

Yet if foreign companies were removed from the American economy, the nation would suffer the loss of one out of every six dollars of GDP, the nation's unemployment rate would soar, states would lose jobs and tax revenues, and communities would lose the opportunity for new schools, roads, parks, cultural support, and businesses that dot the landscape in places such as Buffalo, West Virginia, and Georgetown, Kentucky. Furthermore, were these companies to disappear, there is no assurance that American firms would step in to fill the gap—not when they are putting their focus and dollars into places such as China, India, and Russia, the latest hot spots in the global investment race.

In 2008, even as they pushed for a federal bailout package

on which they said their survival depended, Detroit's struggling auto companies continued to announce investments overseas, including $3 billion Ford said it would spend on operations in Mexico, even though members of the UAW lobbied hard for the work. Even after GM accepted more than $15 billion from the Treasury, it disclosed plans to double the number of cars it builds in Mexico, China, and South Korea. The companies justified these steps by saying they were no longer just American but international companies whose ultimate fate rested just as much on their operations outside the United States as it did on those at home. (To be fair, Ford decided not to take a federal bailout when it became clear it would have to justify its future actions to the Treasury Department and GM said it would build small cars in an American plant.) But justified or not, this decision demonstrated that even in Detroit's darkest hour, there was no sign that the outward flow of jobs and funds would cease anytime soon.

In his bestselling book *The World Is Flat*, author and *New York Times* columnist Thomas Friedman declared that the economy has been leveled by attitudes, technology, and changing social trends. I would argue that on this flattened playing field, Americans are among those who are winning, not losing. Foreign investment makes the country stronger, not weaker. It makes communities better places to live, and it gives Americans a better chance to advance, thrive, and achieve their full potential. In the late years of the Bush administration, when the United States found itself cut off politically from much of the world, foreign investment kept the nation connected, in a very tangible way, to what happened elsewhere.

But make no mistake. Just as foreign investment cannot

support every working American on its shoulders, the American economy cannot expect to sustain itself through foreign investment alone. No matter how much some pundits would wish American companies to have a lock on every dollar earned in the United States, we cannot expect an economy fueled only by American investment—nor should we want one. A nation whose economy is isolated from the ideas and influences outside its shores is one that is doomed to be buffeted by the winds of financial change. American companies need to lead and they need to have faith in American workers and invest in the United States, even as they expand around the world. Foreign investment is not a substitute for this; it is a complement, one that the American economy needs to offer so that the nation can compete, prosper, and, ultimately, remain a leader in the great global race.

Chapter Two

THE
INVISIBLE
WORKER

Let all thoughtful citizens sustain them, for the future of labor is the future of America.

—JOHN L. LEWIS

H ome is not where you live, but where they understand you, wrote Christian Morgenstern, the German poet. For generations, Americans have found it necessary to leave their homes in search of a livelihood and, with it, a better future. During the 1930s and 1940s, more than 250,000 people were forced to migrate from the American South to Detroit, California, and other industrial centers in pursuit of jobs in automobile, aircraft, and military plants, where they worked long hours to sustain their families. As so many Americans who have lost their jobs or had their homes foreclosed upon in the recent downturn know, in times of extreme hardship, leaving one's home in the hope of a better future is sometimes, sadly, simply the only choice.

For Nevada Ryan, that home was Mississippi. A graduate of Mississippi State University with a degree in aerospace engineering, Ryan is descended from a family of crop dusters. Her grandfather, father, mother, and eventually Ryan herself all learned to fly the small fixed-wing aircraft (familiar to viewers of the movie *North by Northwest*) that ply the fields across the South during the growing season. Her family history and early exposure to those nimble little planes sparked in her a lifelong interest in aviation, which led her to get her own private pilot's license and to later study engineering in school.

But when Ryan graduated, there were no engineering jobs available in her home state, so she set off for a job in Atlanta. There, she quickly learned that the common courtesy and friendliness she was accustomed to in Mississippi did not translate across the South. Twice, her car broke down on one of Atlanta's busy highways, leaving her stranded and helpless by the side of the road as traffic roared indifferently by. At home, Ryan said, she would not have waited ten minutes before a passing motorist would lend a hand. "If you break down on the side of the road, somebody will stop and help you and you won't have to fear for your life," she said.

Tired of the cold anonymity and fast pace of the bustling city, Ryan couldn't have been happier when she heard that American Eurocopter, part of the EADS consortium, would be expanding its original facility in Columbus, Mississippi, where it would build rescue helicopters for the U.S. Army. She applied, was hired as a flight test engineer, and was promptly flown to Germany for training. Asked how she and her colleagues felt about owing their livelihoods to a company based overseas, Ryan responded, "I don't think anybody here has a problem with it."

Ryan is just one example of the five million workers across the country who owe their livelihoods to a foreign-owned company. In Ryan's case, a job with a foreign company was an opportunity to move back home and raise her family close to relatives and friends. But whether home is Mississippi or Michigan, Nashville or New York—or even if moving home isn't the goal at all—the point is that foreign companies provide American workers with more than jobs; they provide them with *options*.

The stories of these American workers are rarely told. They have become an invisible American workforce—even though they are spread across the fifty states in sectors ranging from manufacturing to retail to publishing. When we talk about the plight of American workers, we tend to bemoan the plant closings and outsourcing by American companies. But what is rarely spoken is that American workers do have another place to turn.

"When manufacturing spread to towns across America, it brought jobs and a way of life. Working-class families could buy their first home and a piece of the American dream," Barack Obama said during his 2008 campaign. Despite the recent cuts that have devastated American car companies, steelmakers, airlines, financial institutions, and other industries, that way of life is still possible, in part because of foreign companies.

Just ask Judy Flynn, who was given a second chance at a manufacturing career by the foreign-owned American Eurocopter.

ANOTHER CHANCE AT A CAREER

For twenty years, Flynn ran purchasing operations at United Technologies in Columbus, Mississippi, an American company that supplied motors and generators to customers such as General Motors and Chrysler. The plant had opened after Detroit automobile companies and parts suppliers built a wave of new factories in southern states during the 1960s and 1970s, hoping to capitalize on lower wages and operating costs that made southern states an attractive alternative to the Rust Belt. (Part of the bet was that the UAW would not be able to organize the plants, but the UAW managed to do so, anyway.) Flynn had started at the plant on the assembly line and spent ten years assembling motors before she was promoted to an office job and then to purchasing supervisor.

But soon Flynn, who saw every parts order that came into the factory, noticed that requisitions for parts the plant had previously been fulfilling were instead being sent to China. "I had an idea that something was happening globally," she said. Indeed it was. In 1999, United Technologies put its auto parts operation up for sale, and in 2003 closed the plant entirely, putting its two thousand employees out of work.

So when Flynn, the mother of three daughters, with no college degree ("I had 'life experience,' " she said, with a smile) heard that Eurocopter planned to open a facility at the nearby Golden Triangle Regional Airport, she knew right away she'd been given a second chance. Even without a degree, she landed an office job, and after four years at American Eurocopter, worked her way to a position as a supervisor in the materials department. Known to her coworkers as "Miss Judy," Flynn is easy to spot by her bright blue lanyard bearing lapel pins with pictures of American Eurocopter aircraft, which she wears with her company identification card.

Still, for Flynn, as for many of the American Eurocopter employees, the adjustment has not been easy. In the company's first year, turnover was fast and furious as workers struggled with the routine of assembling helicopters. The time-consuming work is as challenging as a skilled trades position, demanding precision, attention to detail, and a reasonable understanding of helicopter mechanics. It was as far from the routine of a typical manufacturing plant as anything could be, which was not what some of the workers had expected. The drop-out rate was high, "mainly driven by the fact of people not knowing very well what we were doing," said Mark Paganini, the chief executive of American Eurocopter.

American Eurocopter executives soon realized something had to be done in order to protect their new investment. Most of the original workers had left, taking what little experience they had with them, and newcomers were making all kinds of mistakes, which were costly given that the helicopters being assembled were used for military rescue missions, where lives were quite literally at stake. But instead of giving up on their workers and replacing them with more experienced foreign transplants (as they easily could have chosen to do), the executives decided to spend more time interviewing and assessing American workers, and to provide more training once they were on the plant floor. Flynn said the attitude at the plant became, "We will help you to succeed—we are determined you will succeed here." Soon, the turnover rate had slowed down, and Americans like Flynn, with no college degree or technical background, were assembling state-of-the-art helicopters.

Factory work might sound dull and unappealing to many Americans, for whom the thought of life on the assembly line conjures images, gleaned from old movies, of dank, windowless rooms packed with thousands of workers performing agonizing, mindless tasks for uninterrupted twelve-hour stretches. But anyone who has ever been employed at a modern factory—

foreign-owned or otherwise—knows that this is no longer the reality.

This is why even some workers fortunate enough to have other alternatives will opt for assembly line or managerial work at a foreign-owned factory; for the many Americans struggling to make ends meet, it is not just a last-ditch option, it's a coveted opportunity.

LIFE ON THE ASSEMBLY LINE

The Howard family—Brian; Stephanie; their sons, Jordan and Dillon; their dog, Scoobie; and a menagerie of other animals, including rabbits, a gecko, and a tree lizard—live in a brand-new three-bedroom house with green shutters in Williamstown, Kentucky, not far from Interstate 75. The custom-built house, the second that the Howards have constructed, is filled with furniture and cabinets made by Brian, an amateur woodworker, himself. Out front, a fountain babbles softly beneath a bright blue Kentucky sky. The neighborhood is dotted with new homes, some of them owned by his coworkers, and the families often take excursions together, racing go-karts or going for drives in the country.

With only a thirty-minute commute to his job, Brian Howard tries to make it home for supper every night and spends his free time coaching his kids' soccer team. Howard met Stephanie, a substitute teacher, in his last year of college at Northern Kentucky University, where he received his degree in business management in 1989. Both were working in an IGA food store and got engaged a few years after they met.

When Howard first heard about the new plant that Toyota planned to build in Georgetown, he immediately sent for the application card. But he hadn't finished college, there was no automotive experience in his background, and he knew little of what to expect from working at a car plant, let alone one by a Japanese company. So he went back to school and got his degree. Now, nearly twenty years later, Howard is a team leader in the paint department at one of the two assembly plants at the Georgetown complex, which also includes an engine plant and employs 7,800 workers. Most of them, like Howard, had college degrees and little experience on an assembly line before they joined the Japanese automaker.

Howard, the son of a schoolteacher and a dog groomer, had the kind of work ethic that is attractive to any employer, American or foreign. He was accustomed to earning his own spending money, even as a boy; he had helped his brothers with their paper routes and had mowed lawns as soon as he was big enough to push a mower. He then took the job at the IGA to earn money for college, working full-time while attending courses. So, the hard work required on the assembly line did not daunt him later on.

Howard was hardly the only one to jump at the chance to work for Toyota. As soon as the state opened the application process, more than 80,000 people submitted cards hoping to be considered for the original 2,000 jobs—40 applicants for every position. "That was one of the most sought-after jobs, even back then," recalled Stephanie. And indeed, every foreign-owned automobile factory that has opened before or since Toyota in Georgetown has received the same kind of reception. For example, when Honda announced in 2007 that it would hire the first 18 people at its factory in Greensburg, Indiana, it received a staggering 20,000 applications.

For Howard, the main attraction at Toyota was the job's pay and benefits—such as health care and a retirement plan (not always standard for hourly workers). He began at about $20 an hour, and now earns roughly $25 an hour, or about $6.50 over the national average ($18.48/hour as of May 2009, according to the Bureau of Labor Statistics). There was also the possibility of an annual bonus, as well as chances for promotions. "The money was the number one draw for me," Howard said. And, "I had a degree in management so I thought there'd be opportunities."

A CONUNDRUM FOR UNIONS

The fair wages and ample opportunities for advancement may help explain why one formidable presence is noticeably absent at many foreign-owned plants: the labor union. Unlike the plants and factories in the northern tier of the United States— many of which are organized by groups such as the UAW, the United Steelworkers, the Teamsters, and the like—some, although not all, foreign-owned operations have been built in southern states with Right To Work laws. (Indiana, Ohio, West Virginia, and Kentucky are not Right to Work states, but the UAW has either not tried, or failed, to organize foreign-owned factories there.) The decision by these companies to put their plants in these states has been subject to great debate among labor activists, politicians, and the workers—both at American and foreign companies—themselves.

On one side of the debate are the many workers, like

Howard, who see no reason to unionize. Antiunion sentiment is barely concealed among the workers and in the towns where some foreign companies have put their plants. Years before Toyota decided to build its factory near Tupelo, Mississippi, for example, civic leaders organized a committee aimed at keeping unions out of local manufacturing plants. The effort was enormously successful; only one factory in town is unionized, and workers at Cooper Tire & Rubber, which has more than 1,200 employees, have voted repeatedly to keep out the rubber workers union.

But why such resistance to organized labor among the workers—especially when unions have hundreds of millions of dollars at their disposal and decades of experience advocating tirelessly for those who have voluntarily or even involuntarily joined their ranks? Gary Chaison, professor of industrial relations at Clark University in Worcester, Massachusetts, said he believed that the problems encountered by the Detroit automakers in recent years have dealt the union movement a serious blow.

For factory workers across the country, unions used to be the sole protector, ensuring competitive wages, adequate benefits, and a measure of job security. But as Detroit auto companies closed scores of plants during the 1980s, '90s, and into this decade, leaving tens of thousands of unionized workers without jobs (the automakers shed a total of 120,000 manufacturing jobs between 2005 and 2008 alone), the influence of the UAW began to dramatically wane. By 2009, the union had lost three out of every four jobs at the Detroit car companies that it had held in 1990. It quickly became undeniably and painfully clear—not only to the thousands of laid-off workers, but to anyone reading the headlines—that the UAW could no longer provide workers with the protection they had come to expect.

The UAW was forced to make unprecedented concessions to Chrysler and GM so they could secure billions of dollars in federal assistance and have any hope of survival. (Both ended up in bankruptcy, regardless.) The writing seemed to be on the wall for the union, whose tight grip on the car companies had come to an end. Even Ford, the one company that did not originally seek federal help, won huge givebacks from the union. There, as at the other companies, workers agreed to accept cuts in pay, pensions, health care, and gave up hard-fought work rules and overtime.

The only solace the union received came from President Obama, who spoke fervently in support of UAW members on the day in April 2009 that he announced the government was putting Chrysler into bankruptcy. But with the UAW so weakened, it perhaps comes as no surprise that many American workers—at homegrown and foreign-owned companies alike—are indifferent, even hostile to their presence. (Case in point: Today, only 12.4 percent of Americans belong to a union, compared with 28 percent in 1954.) For twenty years, Howard has watched the union attempt to organize the Toyota plant. "They have tried since day one," he said, when union organizers gathered at the plant gates, holding out leaflets to workers as they passed by. Most of the cars never stopped. Thus far, the UAW has failed to collect enough signatures from the 7,800 workers at Georgetown to even hold a vote, let alone win one. When asked what he thought unions could bring to the plant, Howard answered, "They can say, 'This is what collective bargaining will do for me. It will bring me a declining workforce and a loss of benefits. It's not going to work out well,' " he said.

To fully understand why Howard and many employees at foreign companies see unions as an unnecessary presence, it's important to understand that the experience of working at a foreign-owned plant or factory bears little resemblance to what workers endured at American-owned plants, particularly in the union's formative years. After all, the UAW was born in large part because the life of an American automobile worker in the 1920s and '30s was at best oppressive and, at worst, dangerous.

Turnover was high—more than 130 percent a year, by some estimates—because the conditions inside his factories were miserable (the main reason Henry Ford offered his famous five-dollar-a-day wage was to ensure a steady supply of labor). The plants were hot and dirty, and the concept of ergonomics was a far-off dream. If a worker was injured, there was no such thing as medical leave; they were patched up and sent back to the assembly line or sent home with no guarantee that their job would be there once they recovered. For minority workers, conditions were even worse; even though Ford was faintly praised for hiring blacks, the plants were segregated, and minorities got the toughest jobs and little chance of a promotion.

Even worse, unimaginable though it might seem today, Ford Motor Company actually tried to keep unions out forcibly with its notorious security squad. Henry Ford's hired thugs not only spied on all of his workers' home lives, but even threatened their lives, as well. In the infamous 1937 Battle of the Overpass at the Rouge factory in Dearborn, Michigan, Ford's security forces attacked and beat a group of labor organizers (men and women alike) during a peaceful protest across a footbridge. Walter Reuther, who became one of the country's most respected labor leaders, was bloodied during the attacks.

But conditions at foreign-owned plants and factories today couldn't be sharper in contrast from the bleak, inhumane conditions experienced at the American factories of yore (miserable images of which have been burned into our brains by old newsreels, headlines, and Depression-era movies). The spaces and equipment are newer and better maintained, and worker safety is the utmost priority. Over the years, the UAW has been engaged in a bitter debate with the foreign companies over their actual safety rates, with the union charging that the companies intimidate their workers into failing to report accidents. But federal statistics show that the lost-day rate—reflecting time off the job, not just individual injuries—at the new plants built by foreign automakers in the United States is generally lower than the rate at Detroit factories.

In other words, in the old days, workers at American-owned plants were treated as though they were barely human, and so a union, in the 1930s and even until the late twentieth century, was a source of protection and the only safe way for them to have their collective voices heard. Back then, once a union like the UAW began to gain at one company, organizers could use its power to demand the same changes and benefits at the next. Pretty soon, the movement caught on, and the UAW's strategy—the threat of costly strikes if it did not get what it wanted—worked for decades, building it into an institution as powerful (until recently) as any of the American automakers.

Besides the better conditions and comparatively better

wages than those paid by American companies, many experts also believe communication can be easier at foreign companies because of the collegial, egalitarian atmosphere and culture of openness on the factory floor. Since the earliest days of American manufacturing, the union has been the workers' only voice to management. If a problem took place, a union rep took it up with a foreman. If a serious issue was at stake, a grievance was filed, and an administrative procedure had to be followed. There was little direct contact between plant management and workers on the floor or elsewhere—workers *needed* the union in order to be heard. In contrast, at the Japanese, German, and Korean plants, communication between assembly line workers and management is actively encouraged; workers have the right to pull on a cord that first slows and then stops the line any time a defect is detected, and all employees, regardless of rank, are consistently asked for their opinions, encouraged to submit suggestions for improvement, and rewarded when their suggestions are adopted.

In short, whether it's the result of cultural differences or simply a greater awareness of the importance of employee satisfaction, workers at foreign-owned plants are treated with a level of respect that has traditionally been absent at American ones. This respect is communicated symbolically as well, in everything from dining options to parking paces. Unlike generations of Detroit factories, where management had (and still has) reserved parking spots up by the door, most foreign companies have a single parking lot, shared by workers and bosses. There is generally only one central cafeteria—no executive dining area— and everyone uses the same gym and childcare facilities. Health benefits and bonuses are the same for blue- and white-collar workers, and there are few private offices for salaried employees and managers. In short, why bother to join a union, many employees reason, when we're already being treated well? As Nevada Ryan said about the prospect of a union in the American Eurocopter plant in Columbus, Mississippi, "If it ain't broke, don't fix it."

Another factor keeping the unions out is the very location of the foreign-owned factories. Most foreign-owned companies have opted to set down roots in southern states, where start-up costs are cheaper and labor is plentiful. But the same economic factors that make the South an attractive place to do business also make it an attractive place to live and work; even though wages in southern states are lower in absolute terms than in Detroit or other urban centers, the cost of living and per capita income in the South are also both much lower. So to many workers, jobs created by foreign employers are seen as an opportunity for a middle-class lifestyle, without the expense or requirements of union membership, and without all the years of struggle.

But it is the promise of a secure job that has been by far the biggest draw for foreign employers and their best defense against unionization. In recent years, as American companies—particularly in the manufacturing and auto sectors—have been shuttering factories and slashing jobs at an alarming rate (U.S. employers cut 3.9 million jobs through May 2009, according to the Labor Department), foreign companies can offer more stable employment even in the face of deep production cuts and slower sales.

Still, while many employed by foreign companies see no need for meddlesome unions, in some towns and companies, sentiment is more mixed. The main factor, perhaps not surprisingly, is pay. While the wages Howard earns at Toyota have afforded him and his family a comfortable lifestyle, the fact remains that the average compensation for a worker at a foreign-owned auto factory is roughly $10 an hour less than at an American-owned plant. According to an analysis by the *New York Times*, the primary difference is not in hourly wages but in benefits provided by union contracts. Workers in UAW-represented plants receive cost-of-living allowances that can add eight dollars or more an hour to wages. They receive more vacation time, broader health-care coverage, and fringe benefits like legal assistance and outside childcare, which the foreign companies may not choose to offer at all. That is why when the subject of the union's latest organizing drive came up at Georgetown, Howard acknowledged that some of his coworkers supported the union's efforts.

Indeed, despite the waning power of unions, especially in the automotive sector, the fact remains that when it comes to pay and benefits, groups like the UAW still do offer workers some protection that foreign-owned companies do not. And, while opponents of unions argue that workers at companies such as Toyota simply don't need union protection, since those companies already treat their workers so well, recent events suggest this might not always be the case. In 2007, for example, an internal company document at Toyota announced the company's intention to cut its employee costs by $300 million through 2011, primarily by cutting wages to coincide with those in the local area, rather than offer a standard rate at all its plants.

By late 2008, Toyota had already instituted a lower wage scale at its newer plants. Workers in San Antonio, for example, earn roughly half what their counterparts receive in George-town, in large part because Texas wage rates were far lower, on average, than those in Kentucky. (It has not yet set wage rates at the new plant in Mississippi but is likely to peg them to local pay, as well.)

That same year, faced with rising health-care costs, Toyota made a change in its health-care plan that raised employees' out-of-pocket expenses and cut the free premiums so that they applied only to employees, not their families. Family members could now receive benefits only if the team member purchased the coverage, a standard practice at many corporations)—another change no union would have taken lying down.

And, in December 2007, when Toyota announced that it would be posting a loss in 2008—for the first time in *seven decades*—it appeared that its workers would need an advocate more than ever, as the company began to temporarily halt production at a number of plants and let temporary workers go. Toyota claimed it would not lay off any permanent workers, in keeping with its pledge in Japan, the United States, and elsewhere to offer lifetime employment to those it hired for full-time jobs. There was plenty of skepticism about the promise: Auto industry experts doubted this vow would hold for long, since it would soon simply prove too expensive to continue paying workers who weren't building vehicles. In the meantime, other foreign, nonunion car companies such as Hyundai and Kia, hit even harder by the weak economy, tight credit, and the resulting drop in sales, responded to the industry downturn by freezing pay for managers.

But any kind of work is better than the prospect of being laid off. Union officials say they know they are up against a difficult opponent in companies like Toyota, and many can respect that. "As a family man I have no resentment for people going to work for foreign companies. Jobs are very important these days, mostly because there aren't enough of them," said Quentin King, the president of UAW Local 1413 in Huntsville, Alabama, not far from the Toyota engine plant, which, like the company's other American factories, is nonunion.

There are cases in which foreign companies have managed fine with union members on board. The steelworkers union is in place at ArcelorMittal, the Indian-owned company that is now the parent of the International Steel Group. The UAW represents workers at Mitsubishi's operations in Illinois, which began as a joint venture with Chrysler, and at NUMMI, the GM-Toyota joint venture in California. Moreover, many of the foreign airlines with operations in the United States employ members of the machinists' union at airports around the country.

Whether foreign-based companies will succumb to unionization remains to be seen. Still, the workers' widespread resistance to it suggests that unions are not likely to be a factor at foreign-owned plants, especially in the automobile industry, for years to come. If anything, the difficult economy will make it harder, not easier, for unions to find an audience. Even though Congress is expected to consider legislation that makes it simpler to hold unionization votes, such a step may not be simple to pull off. Ultimately, it will be the decisions and actions of the foreign companies themselves that will determine whether they can hold on to their workforces. "The best selling point that unions have is that workers in foreign-owned companies are employed at management's largess, that whatever the employer gives the employer can take away, and that without a binding legal contract enforced by a grievance process and arbitration, they have no protection except for what management will let them have," said Professor Chaison.

Unions could have a chance, he said, if the companies institute mass layoffs in a "clearly arbitrary, uncalled for, and unfair manner." But those chances are slim, because management knows that its best weapon against unions in this economy is a job.

Chapter Three

FOREIGN CAPITAL

I feel a recipe is only a theme, which an intelligent cook can play each time with a variation.

—JEHANE BENOIT

In 1919, with America getting back on its feet after World War I, Pierre S. Du Pont, the famous Delaware businessman, faced an uncomfortable reality. Just before the war began, Du Pont had purchased a huge stake in General Motors at the urging of William C. Durant, the company's crafty if mercurial creator. But this was proving to be an unwise investment. As Du Pont watched, with growing frustration, Ford eclipsed General Motors in market share, thanks in large part to the success of one basic product: the Model T. To make matters worse, World War I broke out, forcing auto plants to shift their production to airplanes and armaments (just as they would on a grander scale during World War II), and GM's profits plunged even further.

The industry revved up again in 1919, but Du Pont, who held a 28.7 percent stake in the company, quickly realized that if GM ever hoped to take on Ford, which was bent on global expansion, it needed a major injection of cash. With world economies still struggling after the war, and with American investors carefully considering where they wanted to put their money, "It is felt impossible to raise this new capital through the sale of debenture stock," wrote J. J. Raskob, a close associate of Du Pont, in a letter to the company's finance committee.

But luckily there was an alternative. Rather than seek out another American tycoon, Du Pont had turned to his friends at British Nobels, a branch of Nobel Industries, the explosives company founded in Scotland in 1870 by Alfred Nobel, the man who had found a way to manufacture dynamite. "We are in the fortunate position of having the Nobels keenly interested in this matter," Raskob wrote. The Nobels were not quite as generous as Du Pont hoped, but in May 1920, they purchased more than six hundred thousand shares, or about 4 percent of the company—enough to get GM back on its feet. Thanks to this infusion of capital from the Nobels (and support from the Du Ponts) at a critical time, GM was able to build itself back up and overtake Ford to become the world's biggest automobile company in just over a decade.

This story demonstrates just one of the countless ways in which foreign investment can be a lifeline for a struggling American company. Whether by just taking a small equity stake, as the Nobels did, or by buying up entire businesses or product lines, foreign investment has, over the course of our nation's history, brought many an American company back from the brink of ruin—and saved countless American jobs along the way.

EVERY NOOK AND CRANNY

Americans can easily be forgiven if they don't realize how much foreign investment has taken place under their noses. Yet the breadth and variety of foreign companies doing business in the United States is virtually endless. The Organization for International Investment lists 135 foreign companies as members, all of which have acquired American companies, set up operations of their own in the United States, or entered joint ventures with American companies. Pick an industry, and there will be a major player with a foreign owner or at least part owner—sometimes one that arrived with so little fanfare, many American aren't even aware of its origin.

In the food business, for example, vintage brand names such as Nestlé (Switzerland), Food Lion (Belgium), and Anheuser-Busch (also Belgium) are all owned by companies based overseas. In the clothing and cosmetics industries, a number of the largest companies are foreign owned—such as the French-owned Sephora, the leading retailer of perfumes and cosmetics in the United States, which employs hundreds of American workers in nearly one hundred stores from coast to coast. Even media and publishing, industries that couldn't seem further removed—geographically or culturally—from the manufacturing bastions in the South and Detroit, have numerous examples of owners with foreign roots, such as News Corporation, the global media company controlled by the roughish billionaire Rupert Murdoch. Originally founded in Murdoch's native Australia, News Corp. made its first American acquisitions in newspapers, when it bought the *San Antonio News-Express* in 1973, followed shortly by the infamous *New York Post*, one of the nation's oldest dailies. Pretty soon, Murdoch's empire was branching into the movie business, buying up (in two installments) the studio giant Twentieth Century Fox. In the classic trajectory followed by countless other foreign investors—that is, buying up stakes in a number of existing American companies before launching a brand-new venture of its own—soon News Corp. started up its own TV network, and in 1986 the FOX Broadcasting Company was born. Shedding its Australian roots, News Corp. became a Delaware corporation in 2004 and is now based in New York, where, after a hotly contested and widely publicized struggle with the iconic Bancroft family, it bought its premiere holding, the Dow Jones (publishers of the *Wall Street Journal*) for an estimated $5.6 billion.

Similarly, the German media giant company Bertelsmann, originally founded in 1835 as a printer and publisher of prayer books and hymnals, started buying up American properties in the 1970s. In 1979, it purchased the Arista record label and soon snapped up a series of well-known American publishing and music companies, including Doubleday, Bantam Books, Windham Hill Records, and, in 1998, Random House (the publisher of this book), which now houses the company's entire book publishing operations worldwide.

Sony Corporation, one of Japan's best-known electronics giants, has been making inroads into the United States since the end of World War II, when its founder, Masaru Ibuka, heard about Bell Labs' invention of the transistor during a trip to America and convinced the company to license the use of transistor technology in Japan, where the company began producing transistor radios. By 1955, Sony's models were so popular that the company began exporting them to the United States, where they quickly caught on (by 1968, five million had been sold in the United States alone), making Sony a household name in the American consumer electronics market. However, Sony's other sizable U.S. operations are less known; in the 1980s, Sony made a string of American acquisitions, including CBS Records and Columbia Pictures, and a joint venture, with a number of other investors, to purchase Metro-Goldwyn-Mayer, Inc. (MGM).

Foreign banks, too, operate across the United States, with more than 250 doing business in financial capitals such as New York, Los Angeles, and Miami. Some are little known, such as Banco de Bogotá (which has a branch in New York), and others are as prominent as Barclays Capital, the British financial institution that acquired the main U.S. division and headquarters building of Lehman Brothers, the venerable Wall Street brokerage, during the 2008 financial crisis.

So while the more visible foreign companies such as Toyota or Nissan are perhaps the first to come to mind when most Americans think about foreign investment, companies of all stripes are, in fact, buying up stakes in a wide swath of other industries. This, in turn, creates jobs, not just in manufacturing or urban centers but in all the far reaches of the nation.

Donald Grimes, the University of Michigan economist, admits that Americans, like citizens everywhere, often have a visceral fear of the takeover of an American company by foreign owners. But he is adamant that their reactions are completely off base. He recalled talking to a friend in Illinois who vowed he would no longer drink Budweiser after Anheuser-Busch was acquired in 2007 by InBev, the Belgian beverage company. "I said, 'All you're going to do is cost those Americans their jobs. It's made here, and it's made by American workers,' " Grimes said.

Indeed, that is something to stop and think about. After all, if foreign investment can keep an American company in its hometown and its workers in their jobs, then perhaps its participation is something to be welcomed, not feared.

FLYING HIGH

JetBlue Airways was the darling of the airline industry at the start of the twenty-first century. In 1998, its founder, David Neeleman, had gathered a group of airline executives and investors (including legendary money manager George Soros) to launch an airline built on a simple premise: Put civility back in air travel.

It was a brilliant idea. At that point in time, travelers were miserable (though little did they know just how bad things were about to get—at least back then, an airplane ticket included free baggage check-in, a complimentary hot meal, a pillow and a blanket, and a choice of beverage). Airfares were at record highs, planes were aging and crowded, and carriers frequently canceled flights or forced travelers to suffer lengthy delays.

In 2000, JetBlue set out to change all that. It began to offer frequent, conveniently timed flights, in its brand-new, state-of-the-art Airbus aircraft equipped with seatback TVs, from JFK International Airport in New York to various destinations across the continental United States. Its employees were trained to treat passengers like guests; pilots came out from the cockpit to introduce themselves, crew members were friendly, and snacks and beverages were provided upon request.

Fares were low, with no ticket costing more than $299 each way, and so were JetBlue's costs. Even as the industry was dealt a severe blow by the September 2001 attacks, JetBlue not only survived, it prospered.

In its first five years, the airline grew by 30 percent a year. Each year it added at least a dozen new cities to its system, took on hundreds of new employees, and placed orders for many new aircraft, both Airbus A320 jets and the new E190, a regional jet designed by the Brazilian aircraft manufacturer Embraer. The airline's friendly service landed it atop numerous "best airline" lists, and Neeleman became an industry celebrity, profiled on magazine covers and in books with laudatory titles such as "Blue Streak."

But the happy exterior camouflaged some serious issues, which were soon to surface. For one, JetBlue's growth had burgeoned without the necessary technology or discipline to keep it in check. When a snowstorm socked JFK Airport on Valentine's Day, 2007, miring JetBlue's planes in ice and stranding hundreds of passengers on runways or ramps for as long as ten hours, Neeleman turned from hero to scapegoat overnight. He was excoriated by the press, lampooned by David Letterman and Jay Leno, and forced to deliver groveling apologies on national TV and YouTube. JetBlue's board subsequently removed him as chief executive, and he later left the chairman's job as well.

But even after his ousting, things were still not looking good for JetBlue. The snowstorm came on top of two straight years of losses for the company, whose stock had lost four-fifths of its value. By late 2007, as oil prices reached $100 a barrel, bringing the airlines to their knees, it became clear that JetBlue needed a savior. But the airline industry was stunned by the company that came to its rescue in December 2007: Lufthansa, the German airline, with a $430 million investment deal that helped JetBlue put together half a billion dollars in capital just when the company needed it most.

Lufthansa, the world's fifth largest airline, had rarely been mentioned when analysts on Wall Street speculated about who would come to JetBlue's aid. For one thing, it already had an American partner in United Airlines. For another, Lufty, as it was affectionately known in the industry, was facing challenges in Europe, where it was having trouble keeping up with Air France and KLM Royal Dutch Airlines, which had joined forces to become the world's biggest airline. Analysts had thought Continental, which had managed to avoid the financial problems that sent four of the six biggest airlines into bankruptcy during the years after the September 2001 attacks, or American Airlines, the nation's biggest carrier, seemed the most solid prospects to strike a deal with JetBlue.

The idea of a foreign savior hadn't occurred to JetBlue executives, either. Thus, David Barger, who succeeded Neeleman as chief executive, was surprised when he received a message in October 2007 saying that Lufthansa's chief executive, Wolfgang Mayrhuber, wanted to meet with him to discuss taking a stake in his airline. When he received the call, Barger was on a business trip in South Korea and about to fly home to New York over the Pacific. Instead, he headed west to Frankfurt.

The two men were acquaintances who had met periodically over the years at industry conferences. But at this dinner, Mayrhuber wasted no time with small talk. Lufthansa, like the rest of the industry, had watched JetBlue's birth and infancy with interest. In it, Mayrhuber saw a new opportunity. Thanks to a new treaty, called Open Skies, which had loosened some of the restrictions that kept American and European airlines from flying to one another's airports, a stake in JetBlue would allow Lufthansa to add routes to New York, cashing in on the fact that the United States and Caribbean—the same places served by JetBlue—were popular vacation destinations for Germans. "Kennedy is a second Heathrow," Mayrhuber said later. "It shouldn't be undervalued."

In JetBlue, Mayrhuber also saw the opportunity to study American operations, so different from the rule-laden processes that his airline had to follow in Europe. In fact, the chance to get inside an American start-up was his primary motivation, he explained; the chance to capitalize on his investment was secondary. "A financial investment in JetBlue is something interesting, but it wouldn't have been sufficient," he said. "We wanted something of strategic importance for the two companies."

For JetBlue, the purchase was not just strategic, it was a saving grace. It helped the airline raise money from other investors, and it provided cash just before fuel prices spiked to an all new high in 2008. It preserved nearly twelve thousand American jobs, at a time when other airlines were announcing thousands of layoffs, and gave an American company the chance to stabilize itself and, eventually, to keep growing.

SAVING MORGAN STANLEY

The summer of 2008 was nothing less than a living hell for the country's investment banks. With the housing market in collapse, jobs disappearing, the recession in full swing (even if economists had yet to admit it), and venerable institutions such as Bear Stearns, Merrill Lynch, and Lehman Brothers either dissolved or bankrupt (not to mention all the dozens of smaller banks who had closed their doors, as well), the outlook for Wall Street was very grim, indeed. The rolls of investment banks, which once dominated American finance and dictated the direction of global capital, had suddenly shrank to only two main players: Morgan Stanley and Goldman Sachs.

For years, the two had been the envy of Wall Street. They used billions of investors' dollars to land the most lucrative deals the financial world had to offer. They arranged billions of dollars in mergers, brokered major acquisitions around the world, and enabled numerous issues of new stock in every imaginable sector.

But in 2008, all that came crashing down. Confidence in the investment banks, whose balance sheets were torn asunder by the erosion of the home mortgage business, reached a new low, and as property values plunged, clients couldn't pull their money out fast enough. The remaining banks, rightly terrified they would join the ever-growing ranks of Bear Stearns, Lehman, and other vanished institutions, began looking for a savior.

Morgan Stanley, which was founded in 1935 by Henry Morgan and Harold Stanley, found that savior in Mitsubishi UFJ Financial Group, Japan's largest commercial bank and one of the main companies of the Mitsubishi Group, whose vast holdings include the eponymous car company, the camera maker Nikon, and Kirin Brewery.

In September 2008, Mitsubishi UFJ (which had $1.1 trillion in bank deposits, making it the second richest global bank), paid $9 billion for a 21 percent stake in Morgan Stanley, a deal that included $3 billion for Morgan Stanley common stock and

$6 billion for preferred shares. The deal came just in the nick of time. Since the spring of 2008, the value of Morgan Stanley's stock had plummeted by nearly half, to about $25, and with the economy worsening by the day, it was in danger of dropping much lower, and fast. Luckily for John J. Mack, Morgan Stanley's chief executive officer, the deal provided the firm with the liquidity it needed to remain independent and to survive the transition into its new future as a commercial bank. As Michael de la Merced, a coauthor of the *New York Times'* DealBook blog, told me, "Morgan Stanley in October was dying from what amounted to a run on the bank. Selling a stake to Mitsubishi gave the firm vital capital that helped it survive."

In another era, investors might have looked askance at a Japanese infusion, fearful of one of the last standing banks (which was, after all, now holding a good portion of our nation's coffers) becoming in any way beholden to foreign interests. But Morgan Stanley had already shown it would not be compromised by foreign help. In December 2007, it had sold $5 billion in shares to the China Investment Corporation, the country's sovereign wealth fund, giving the Chinese government a 9.9 percent stake in the company, to no ill effect; and, in fact, both Citigroup and UBS had recently taken similar steps—Citigroup selling a 4.9 percent stake to Abu Dhabi's investment arm, and UBS selling a stake to the government of Singapore and an unnamed Middle East investor—with equally uncompromising results.

Obviously, the Mitsubishi deal was critically important for the survival of Morgan Stanley, especially at a time when so many of its competitors were so down. But Merced told me that the deal had as much meaning for the Japanese bank, which has holdings in twenty-eight other companies, including Morgan Stanley. "Mitsubishi is, or at least was, in the process of expanding to foreign markets, and gaining a stake in a sterling name like Morgan Stanley benefits it tremendously," Merced said. Meanwhile, the stability provided by the investment helped Morgan Stanley secure $10 billion in federal bailout money and allowed Morgan Stanley to begin the process of not only paying back those funds and rebuilding itself, but of rebuilding investor confidence in the banking system in general. So even though some Americans might have preferred the bank to have looked to American, rather than foreign capital in its hour of need, the fact of the matter was, at the time, such capital simply didn't exist.

FIAT LENDS CHRYSLER A HAND

By Inauguration Day 2009, another quintessentially American name was seeking a foreign rescuer: Chrysler. Just seventeen months before, Cerberus Capital Management, an investment fund, had touted its purchase of Chrysler, which had been put up for sale by the German automaker DaimlerChrysler, as a long-awaited return of the company to American ownership. Chrysler had been on a roller-coaster ride for most of its eighty-five-year history, particularly over the past three decades; ever since the late 1970s, its lows have been low, and its highs have indeed been high.

In 1979, Lee Iacocca became nothing less than an American folk hero after rescuing the company from bankruptcy, albeit with help from federal loan guarantees and concessions from dealers, suppliers, and the UAW. Within a few years, Chrysler had not only paid back the money it owed its creditors, it was well on the road to growth, thanks to the popularity of its new minivans, which were perfectly attuned to the needs of the exploding suburban populace, and its economical K-cars. As hard as it may be to imagine today, Chrysler was so successful in the 1990s, it became the darling of the automobile industry, catching the eye of none other than Daimler-Benz, the owner of Mercedes. When the two companies merged in 1998, the deal was hailed as having created the first truly global automaker, paving the way for other multinational collaborations, such as the arrangement between Renault of France and Nissan of Japan. These mega deals also spurred Ford to buy Volvo and Land Rover, and GM to take stakes in a series of foreign companies, including Fiat.

Under German leadership, Chrysler soared again in the middle of the 2000s, its profits and market share boosted by such cars as the 300C, a powerful sedan aimed at urban buyers, and its variety of Jeeps and pickups. Nevertheless, Daimler's German shareholders, who had always complained that Chrysler, with its erratic quality reputation and penchant for discounts, tarnished the Mercedes image, relentlessly pushed Daimler to unload the company. In 2007, they finally got their way, as Cerberus Capital Management stepped up to the plate.

No matter what German shareholders might have thought of Chrysler, Cerberus, which had made millions buying and selling companies of all stripes and was far less concerned with brand image than with bottom lines, saw the purchase as an attractive opportunity. In hindsight, though, Cerberus's move seemed ill-advised. For one thing, gas prices were rising at the time, a clear indication that buyers would soon be trending toward fuel-efficient cars, not the big vehicles that still dominated Chrysler's lineup. And in what should have been another bright red flag, the previous winter, Chrysler's plants had churned out more than one hundred thousand vehicles for which its dealers still did not have orders. The cars sat piled up on lots around Detroit in a painful reminder, to anyone flying in or out of Metro airport, of how fast and far the U.S. automakers had fallen. Still, Cerberus insisted that Chrysler was a long-term investment and that it was not daunted by a little overstock or by the prospect of a difficult car market. But, lo and behold, a year later, the Chrysler roller coaster was once again headed for a nosedive.

In fall 2008, auto sales fell to the worst levels in a quarter century, due to the banking crisis, a freeze on credit, instability in the job market, and the subsequent drop in consumer spending. Robert L. Nardelli, the former Home Depot chief executive brought in by Cerberus to run Chrysler, made a dire prediction: If Chrysler did not receive a federal bailout, the company could be out of business in months. After a nasty inquisition in front of Congress (discussed in detail in chapter 10), Chrysler was eventually awarded $4 billion in assistance. But there was a condition: Chrysler (and GM, which received $9 billion in bailout money), had to prove that it had a viable plan for recovery. And in order to do so, Chrysler had to find partners willing to assure its future.

Enter Fiat. Like Chrysler, the Italian automaker had experienced its own roller-coaster ride in recent years. In the 1980s, it had ranked as Europe's biggest automaker and was one of the first European companies to open plants in China, arriving in the days before the country's Communist government encouraged Western investment. But, also like Chrysler, its cars were plagued by poor quality (its name, jokesters quipped, stood for "Fix It Again, Tony"), and in 1983, after repeatedly landing at the bottom of quality surveys, it ultimately was forced to pull out of the American market (its Alfa Romeo brand hung on for a few more years but was essentially extinct in America by 1994).

The company faced problems in Europe, too. Toyota and Honda had begun to build cars at plants in France and Britain, threatening Fiat's customer base and market share, and Volkswagen had recently undergone a turnaround, bumping Fiat from the top spot among European carmakers. Plus, Fiat's strategy of diversifying beyond cars had bogged down the company with more businesses than it could handle.

By 2004, the Agnelli family, which ran the Italian carmaker, was desperately in need of fresh blood. They found it in an unlikely chief executive: Sergio Marchionne, a Canadian-Italian businessman trained in accounting and law. Turns out, this unusual pedigree was just what the company needed; Marchionne soon transformed Fiat from a bloated conglomerate into a leaner, more focused competitor by selling off its airline, insurance, and banking divisions while broadening Fiat's automotive reach with big hits, like the Fiat 500, a new version of the small car that many Italians had purchased once their economy finally recovered after World War II.

Encouraged by his success reinvigorating Fiat on its home turf, Marchionne was now anxious to reenter the American market. He soon saw his opportunity in Chrysler. Talks to buy up shares in the company began quietly in the summer of 2008, and on the morning of Barack Obama's inauguration, Detroit woke up to learn that Chrysler had once again linked up with a foreign investor.

For Fiat, the deal carried as little risk as possible. It would take 35 percent of Chrysler, for next to nothing, and in turn, it would be permitted to sell its vehicles at Chrysler dealers, just as Fiat dealers around Europe could sell Chrysler models. There was also an implicit understanding that if the deal worked, Fiat might eventually take a majority share in the company. (The terms eventually were adjusted.)

While this might have seemed like a raw deal for Chrysler, it wasn't, for one significant reason: A partner such as Fiat could help secure the bailout money (and reassure the American tax-payer he would get that money back) that was so critical to the future of the company and its tens of thousands of workers, whose ranks had already dwindled by half, or more than twenty-five thousand, since 2007. In other words, the partnership could secure "the long-term viability of Chrysler brands in the market-place, sustaining future product and technology development for our country and building renewed consumer confidence, while preserving American jobs," Nardelli said. Within months, Nardelli was bidding Chrysler good-bye, and Chrysler faced the ultimate challenge to its survival: bankruptcy court. President Obama announced in April 2009 that Chrysler would seek Chapter 11 protection, using federal money, and that a new company would be created to be jointly owned by the Treasury, the UAW's health care fund, and Fiat. At the outset, Fiat would own 20 percent, but that could rise to 35 percent, and the new company would be run by its CEO, Marchionne.

For Marchionne, the arrangement was a bit of a homecoming. He had earned his MBA at the University of Windsor, Ontario, just across the river from Detroit. And Fiat had courted Chrysler before: In 1990, the company had almost pulled off a merger with Chrysler, only to see the deal fall apart just before it became final. The two companies seemed almost destined to join forces. But, Marchionne stressed, no one should expect Fiat to wave a magic wand and pull off a Chrysler turnaround; its executives would have to do the hard work themselves. "I think Chrysler has all the prerequisites to survive," Marchionne said. "But the bigger issue is, what does it look like two or three years from now? It's not as if Fiat is going to show up and Cinderella is going to be magically turned into something else."

Why, given Chrysler's uncertain future, would Fiat want to tap into the bankrupt American company? For one thing, it gave the company access to Chrysler's extensive network in the United States—the kind of network that, as automakers from Honda and Toyota to BMW and Mercedes-Benz had learned, can take a foreign company years to develop. Plus, it was quite simply a cheap, quick, and virtually risk-free venture into a market that could be incredibly profitable once the U.S. economy recovered. To Marchionne, that made the prospect of returning to America worth it. "We're not doing this because we're Good Samaritans," Marchionne said. "We're willing to take a risk on investing technology and time to help Chrysler come back to life and bring value to Fiat shareholders."

In short, the deal was a win-win; Fiat was also taking a minimal risk on the American economy just when it needed the moral support that foreign investment could provide, even if no euros or dollars changed hands. While moral support may not seem like much, the importance of investor confidence should never be underestimated. When companies such as Lufthansa, Mitsubishi, and Fiat partner with American firms, they bring to the table so much more than just capital; they bring a show of faith—faith in our companies, our economy, and our future. Beyond saving tens of thousands of American jobs or preserving fledgling American institutions, they are shoring up the American image, by telling the world that we are still open for business. So while the role of these stakeholders may not be as transformative—or as visible—as that of some of the other foreign investments discussed throughout this book, these firms are, without a doubt, still providing hope for American companies, American communities, and American workers—at a time when so little hope exists.

Chapter Four

NOT
IN MY
BACKYARD

*You cannot protect something by building a fence
around it and thinking that this will help it survive.*

—WIM WENDERS

Throughout the centuries, countries have seized upon two methods of defending themselves from threats from abroad: military force and political rhetoric. Both are used to battle invaders—whether to the nation itself, to its economy, or simply to the collective national ego. In more cases than not, both stem from perhaps the most elemental and fundamental of human emotions: fear. Because, in truth, foreignness scares people—whether that fear is rational or not.

In some cases, foreign investment stirs up fears that are both visceral and rational. Consider the case of the public uproar over the 2006 attempted takeover of five American port terminals by the United Arab Emirates–owned company Dubai Ports World (DPW), the battle by EADS of Europe for a $35 million military contract, or the bid by the China National Offshore Oil Corporation (CNOOC) for the American oil company Unocal. In these instances, the fear was for our safety. To some Americans, the notion of allowing foreign companies (particularly, in the case of DPW, an Arab one) largely unfettered access to our ports, our oil supply, and the plans to fuel our fighter jets seemed risky if not downright dangerous.

But other times, this fear of foreign investment has nothing to do with our physical safety; it's a fear shared among politicians, pundits, commentators, and ordinary citizens alike that foreign companies who do business in the United States are a threat to American jobs, American businesses, and, in fact, to the American way of life. When we fear that our economy is being invaded, our solution is often to close our hearts, our minds, and our doors to companies from abroad.

Historically, this has generally taken the form of protectionist rhetoric; in tough economic times, our fears are heightened and our inclination for protectionism grows only stronger. This is why, as the economy has taken an ugly turn in recent years and employment has risen to the highest levels in decades, cries of "Buy American!" have grown only louder in some circles. Most economists agree that such a solution is completely misguided, because, as we have seen, rather than putting our homegrown companies out of business, as protectionists fear, foreign-owned firms in fact employ the very workers that our own companies can no longer afford to sustain.

Only three months after taking office, President Obama, although appearing to the world as a pragmatist on trade, showed that he was behind the home team. "If you are considering buying a car, I hope it will be an American car," he said (a statement that GM's chief executive, Fritz Henderson, may have preferred he not make. Asked on *Meet the Press* a few weeks before if he wanted the president to make such a statement, Henderson replied, "I think the consumer should buy exactly what kind of car they think meets their needs and that excites them. And as I look at it, it's our job to make sure we provide that, not necessarily have it mandated or otherwise encouraged").

"What is 'Buy American,' anyway?" economist Donald Grimes asked. "Is it buying from General Motors, because General Motors was started as an American company? If you buy from GM and it's made in Canada or Mexico, is it buying American? It's a question that people aren't really asking themselves." As the writer and journalist Patricia Marx aptly pointed out in a March 16, 2008, piece in the *New Yorker*, products are made by so many companies, based in so many countries all over the world, that "buying American" is hardly a cut-and-dried proposition anymore. She wrote, "The production of this paragraph was not outsourced to the Philippines or Mexico. It was written, punctuated, and fact-checked in the U.S.A. It was however, composed on a laptop computer that was manufactured by Lenovo, a company in which the Chinese government owns a twenty-seven percent share. . . . The writer is American but also Russian and Romanian. Her ideas derive partially from Adam Smith, the Scottish moral philosopher and political economist. A coffeemaker made by the German company Braun was tangentially involved."

While many critics of foreign investment may deny charges of xenophobia, it can't be denied that, more often than not, their attitude toward foreign companies who come to do business in the United States is "not in my backyard."

PROTECTIONIST RHETORIC:
A COST OF DOING BUSINESS

Many foreign companies have experienced some form of protectionist sting as they have expanded into the United States. Sometimes the fervor flares quickly and just as quickly dies, as it did when a subsidiary of Indian-owned Tata bought Tyco Global Network, an American telecommunications company, in 2005. Other times the rhetoric envelopes a company and causes enough problems to derail a major American investment, as when protectionist sentiment pressured Chinese Haier into giving up its bid for Maytag, the appliance manufacturer that outfitted homes across America with washers, dryers, and refrigerators for the better part of the twentieth century. In the most extreme cases, protectionist sentiment can lead to shifts in government policy, such as the voluntary restraint agreement in the early 1980s that limited sales of Japanese cars in the United States.

Nevertheless, this backlash is a cost of doing business for global companies, who encounter it not just in America but in many parts of the world. "In any country, foreign investment tends to be an emotive issue," said Alan Rosling, Tata's globalization chief. "It would certainly happen in India, if GE came along and acquired an Indian company." Rosling, who is British, felt there was an "almost racist" reaction in Europe when Lakshmi Mittal, an Indian entrepreneur, made a hostile bid for Arcelor, the Luxembourg-based steel company, which was actually a combination of French, Spanish, and Luxembourg companies, in 2006. The proposal by the third richest man in the world was completely unexpected and left government officials in shock. Luxembourg's prime minister, Jean-Claude Juncker, vowed that his government would block the deal. "We cannot recognize an industrial concept in Mittal's proposals," he declared. France's finance minister, Thierry Breton, also dismissed the idea, saying he had never seen "such a badly prepared takeover bid." Discussion went on for months, with bitter exchanges in India and Europe, until the two companies finally merged, unhappily, in June 2006. Likewise, the British media raised an uproar when Tata emerged as the leading bidder for the fabled Land Rover and Jaguar brands (even though Jaguar had been in American hands for seventeen years and Land Rover for more than a decade).

Of course, this knee-jerk, visceral response to foreign investment is all too common in the United States as well. "The U.S., because of its size, is more inward looking than some other countries," Rosling said. That is evident just by switching on a cable television news show, listening to politicians in Washington, or even soliciting the views of one's neighbor, many of whom, seeing a threat to our companies and our workers where none exists, misperceive the role that foreign companies have in the American economy. Indeed, for foreign companies doing business in the United States, protectionist sentiment is a bitter pill to swallow and a huge barrier to overcome. No one knows this better than Tata of India.

EIGHT O'CLOCK SOMEWHERE IN THE WORLD

Few sights are more familiar on American supermarket shelves than the red, gold, and black bag of Eight O'Clock Coffee. Introduced in 1859 by the Great American Tea Company (which later became known as the Great Atlantic and Pacific Company or just the A&P), Eight O'Clock Coffee is one of the oldest products in the country. Its clever name, coined in 1919, came from research that showed coffee was most frequently consumed at 8 a.m. and 8 p.m. Its popularity owes much to a clever marketing campaign centering on the fact that, as a digital clock on the company's Web site now declares, "It's always eight o'clock" somewhere in the world. (Older consumers might remember the Eight O'Clock Coffee billboard in New York's Times Square, erected in 1933, where a gigantic cup of Eight O'Clock Coffee let off real steam on a regular basis.)

But those who view Eight O'Clock as just another American brand of coffee such as Folgers or Maxwell house might be surprised to find the words "A TATA Enterprise" in small print on every bag of original, decaffeinated, french vanilla, and hazelnut sold. Since 2005, Eight O'Clock Coffee has been owned by the Tata Group, India's second largest conglomerate. Some would be even more surprised to learn that shoppers can find even more products owned by Tata just down the aisle.

Tata is the owner of Good Earth Tea, the California-based organic tea company whose flavors include Cocoa Chai and Rainforest Red, and Tetley Tea, the British brand it purchased in 2000. What's more, a shopper who drove up to the grocery store in a Jaguar or a Land Rover would be riding in a vehicle now produced by Tata, and farther afield, a traveler who registers at the Taj Hotel in Boston or the Campton Place in San Francisco is a guest of the Indian-owned company.

Tata, based in Mumbai, owns ninety-eight companies in seven business sectors. It operates in more than eighty-five countries on six continents and produces everything from beverages to steel to chemicals to paint. It has nearly twenty thousand employees in the United States, in operations from coast to coast, and offers services that range from consulting to beverage sales to information technology. In 2007, the company's yearly revenue was $62.5 billion, and it is still growing.

Yet, it's safe to say that the average American knows little about Tata. There are no ads extolling Tata's community activities during Sunday broadcasts of *Meet the Press*, like the kind run by Toyota, no Tata billboard lighting up Times Square. Although it has snapped up some beverage companies, Tata has not pursued any big iconic American brands, like InBev, the Belgian company that bought Anheuser-Busch in 2008. And unlike Haier, the Chinese appliance maker, which has declared its intent to someday control 10 percent of the American home-goods market, Tata has not touted specific market-share goals for the businesses it has in the United States, although it has internal plans for each unit.

For all his prominence, at seventy-one, Ratan Tata, in sharp contrast with other global business leaders such as Jack Welch of General Electric or Richard Branson of Virgin Atlantic, is something of an enigma in the business world, living alone in Mumbai with his dogs. Not for him is the flamboyant life of a Lee Iacocca or a Ted Turner, with their multiple marriages and extravagant spending: Tata never married, has no heirs, and would be able to pass unnoticed, except perhaps by the staff, in one of his luxury hotels. Both Tata's public persona and his approach to doing business in the United States has been deliberately stealth, in large part to avoid the public hostility that his company has faced in the past.

Tata Group first became entangled in protectionist debate

earlier this decade, when, just as the company was beginning its efforts to expand its American holdings, a series of American firms made the highly publicized decision to outsource a substantial amount of office work, such as call centers, to Indian companies. Hearing British-tinged Indian accents when they phoned up with questions about their credit cards touched a nerve with many consumers, and Tata became a scapegoat for every job that had ever been shed in the United States. "We were the poster child for the outsourcing of jobs," said Rosling.

In October 2005, when Tata Technologies purchased INCAT, a global engineering and product development company based in the United Kingdom, it experienced another nasty sting of public wrath. Over the years, INCAT had picked up an impressive international client list, from Boeing to Chrysler to Mercedes-Benz, and by 2004, its operations stretched from North America (including a Michigan headquarters a stone's throw from Chrysler's offices) to Europe to Japan. A year later, when INCAT was put up for sale, and Tata, on the prowl for companies to enhance its engineering capabilities, snapped it up, the protectionist outcry was shocking. "When we were first acquired, there were a lot of concerns that, 'The Indians are coming! The Indians are coming!'" said Warren Haines, the company's chief executive, who is based at the offices of what is now named Tata Technologies in Troy, Michigan. "People thought they would take the profits back to India and leave the Americans with not very much to go on."

Another arm of Tata's business that has had to work to overcome Americans' fear and suspicion—tinged with, one could argue, more than a bit of racism—is Tata's hotel group, whose

American holdings include three of the country's most famous hotels: the former Ritz-Carlton in Boston, which has been renamed the Taj; the Campton Place Hotel in San Francisco, and the Pierre Hotel in New York. All three are well-known properties with cultural significance in their cities.

In Boston, generation after generation of blue bloods have held weddings, debutante balls, and christening ceremonies in the stately ballroom and meeting rooms of the Ritz, which overlooks Boston Common. It was the type of hotel where mothers took daughters (as mine did) for their first proper lunch or afternoon tea, the sort of place where society couples spent the first night of their honeymoon before jetting off to Europe or sailing to Bermuda. So it's not entirely shocking that in 2007, the prospect of an Indian company purchasing such an iconic and historic property sent ripples of concern among some circles in Boston; the name change alone seemed to shake Boston traditionalists to their core. "There was the expectation that we'd set up a samosa stand in the lobby," said David Good, who heads Tata's U.S. corporate office.

But in the end Tata won over even the bluest of the blue bloods, thanks in no small part to the special efforts the company took to preserve the original character of the venerable landmark—while improving it at the same time. For example, the Taj retained the signature cobalt blue and crystal chandeliers that for decades tinkled quietly in its second-floor dining room while adding luxurious amenities such as butlers, who could run baths or stoke wood-burning fireplaces. To cultivate further goodwill in the community, the Taj managers built relationships with homeowners associations in Back Bay and Beacon Hill, and donated money to the Emerald Necklace Conservancy, a nonprofit group that helps maintain Boston Common in front of the hotel.

"The local community really is key," said Raymond Bickson, the chief executive of Tata's hotel group, who also made sure that key staff members remained in place so that local residents would see familiar faces when they came in the door or visited the dining room. Ultimately, the strategy worked. Said Good, "I think people realize now that we aren't here to Indianize; we're here to Americanize. We are employing a lot of Americans."

Tata's executives were right to tread carefully, given that the murmurs of concern about the Ritz came on the heels of a series of bids by Indian companies for foreign properties, some of them hostile, and Indian-owned companies weren't exactly perceived favorably in the public eye. One of those purchases even caused the company's most notable political skirmish to date: the debate in Washington that surrounded Tata's purchase (by its VSNL subsidiary) of Tyco Global Network, an international telecommunications and Internet company.

In a way, the public outcry over these ventures ended up being a valuable lesson for the company; they made Tata officials realize that attempting to fly under the radar, or remain invisible, was no longer a viable strategy. Instead, they would have to work hard to be accepted in the United States and elsewhere as participants, not aggressors. "The only thing you can do is earn the right to be perceived as a responsible owner of a company," Rosling said. To this end, Tata's consulting arm, TCS, has begun donating fifty cents of every dollar of American profits to charities such as the March of Dimes and the American

Cancer Society and to community organizations in the thirty-six cities where it operates, said Surya Kant, president of TCS North America.

Having a low profile can come at a cost when it comes to their consumer arm, too. Barbara Roth, the chief executive officer of Eight O'Clock Coffee and a veteran marketing executive, says she wishes Tata's visibility in the United States was higher. As a brand name, "Tata doesn't, in the short term, bring us anything" when it comes to convincing stores to stock its products. "We don't have the Kraft sales force behind us, the Proctor sales force behind us. When we go to retailers, we have to explain who we are, and say that they will see more activity" from us in coming years, she said.

Rosling said the company knows it needs to do more to hone its public image. "We have been in the United States for sixty years but it is only in last five, six, or seven years that we have been here as an investor, an employer, or a corporate citizen, rather than a trader," he said. "It is relatively early in our time in the United States. Hopefully we can demonstrate we are a responsible employer." Because for Tata, like any other foreign-owned company, doing successful business in the United States depends not just on being noticed, but on being accepted.

"MADE IN JAPAN"

When Toyota entered the American market in 1957, residual anger over the war in the Pacific was still sharply felt. Japanese products, which had not yet achieved the quality for which they would later be known, were derided as cheap and shoddy, and "Made in Japan" was as much a joke as a stamp of origin.

Detroit auto companies, who controlled more than 90 percent of the American car market, and consumers alike scoffed at the small Toyopet models that Toyota brought to the United States.

But over the past twenty-five years, Toyota has achieved something that the business world might have considered impossible. Despite the lingering anti-Japanese sentiment, the cries of "Buy American" that have long reverberated through the populace, and the political wrath that the company received in Washington only a generation ago, Toyota has built itself into the world's biggest auto company, and the second biggest in the United States.

Like Tata's, Toyota's American journey into the United States began with baby steps, but unlike Tata, those steps were in the full glare of a spotlight. Toyota did not jump into American manufacturing by opening its own factory, as other Japanese companies did during the 1980s, or as Haier did in 1999. Instead, Toyota hedged its bets and began a joint venture in California with GM, then one of America's most esteemed—and most profitable—companies. "They partnered with GM because they were scared," said Jeffrey K. Liker, the University of Michigan professor and author of a number of bestselling books about Toyota. Whether that fear was justified or not, it took years, and push from the voluntary restraint agreement, for Toyota to open its own factory this side of the Pacific. By the time it began building cars in Georgetown, Kentucky, in 1988, Toyota was years behind other foreign carmakers such as Nissan, Mazda, and Honda. But its slower approach paid off in the end, partly because it helped to neutralize the xenophobia of some of its critics, who feared that the Japanese company posed a threat to the Big Three automakers, which, to be fair, it probably did.

In retrospect, some of Toyota's success in fending off protectionist sentiment was due to timing. In the mid-1990s, as Toyota was putting its growth plans together, Detroit companies were enjoying a resurgence. They had hit on SUVs, minivans, and pickups as their keys to a rebound after a deep sales decline early in the decade, while Japanese companies actually saw their sales go down in this period, due to the strong yen and their lack of big vehicles. Detroit and its champions were confident that the Japanese, including Toyota, had been defeated, and so they let down their guard. By the time they realized their mistake, Toyota and the other companies already had expansion plans in place.

Once it got going in the United States, Toyota's rapid growth essentially took place under Detroit's nose and without Detroit's realization—until it was far too late. In 2003, Toyota outsold Chrysler for the first time, and in 2007, it passed Ford to become the country's second biggest car company. By early next decade, once its Mississippi factory opens, Toyota is expected to be able to build 2.5 million cars and trucks a year in the United States, far more than GM, Ford, and Chrysler (if they even still exist by then). Jay Rockefeller, West Virginia's veteran Democratic senator, summed it up best when he told me that "Compared with a Detroit automaker, their future is bigger."

Toyota's market capitalization in 2008 was $163.84 billion—equal to the gross domestic product of Shanghai and one hundred times the value of GM's outstanding shares, which had plummeted as the automaker slipped closer to bankruptcy. In North America alone, Toyota earned an operating profit of $18.2 billion from 2002 to 2007, a period when Detroit companies collectively lost tens of billions of dollars, much of it in one-time charges taken to reflect the deterioration of their American operations. The string of success ended only when Toyota was hit by the same slump in 2008 that afflicted virtually all of the world's auto companies. It lost $3.9 billion worldwide and began to cut costs across its operations (but, by comparison, that was less than Ford lost in the fourth quarter of 2008 alone).

Yet despite—or perhaps because of—its overwhelming success in the U.S. market, backlash toward Toyota continues. One oft-cited criticism of the company is that Toyota's workers are not unionized; in labor circles, any nonunion factory remains a threat to American workers and to a dwindling way of American life. In the fall of 2008, as the Detroit companies approached Congress on their hands and knees (or rather on their private jets) pleading for bailouts, much was made of the fact that Toyota pays $45 per hour in wages and benefits to each of its workers, compared to GM's $73. (The bulk of the discrepancy was attributed to GM's considerably larger pool of retired workers; when adjusted for this and other factors, the difference in pay was estimated to be about $10 an hour.) This was cited as a sign of Detroit's excesses, but to some Americans it also signaled the infuriating fact that Toyota was simply getting away with paying its workers less.

So no matter how many applicants line up for jobs at Toyota's American plants, no matter the reception it receives from local communities or the incentives it is offered from states seeking investments, company executives understand that an emotional reaction lies just beneath the surface. "It's important for Toyota to recognize that whatever we do, some people will not recognize that things have changed. We need to have a guard up against that," said George Borst, CEO of Toyota Financial Services, and a longtime company executive.

A GOAL BEYOND REACH

In the mid-2000s, Haier, the Chinese appliance maker, reached a similar conclusion when it discovered just how quickly protectionist sentiment can derail a foreign company's plan for growth. From the time it set its sights on the American market in the 1990s, Haier knew that it would have to make a significant acquisition in order to achieve its goal of holding a 10 percent share, and it soon concluded that such an acquisition would have to come from an established American brand. It thought it had the perfect candidate in Maytag.

Founded in 1893 as an agricultural implements company, Maytag shifted to washing machines in 1907 with its first model, the Pastime. By 1924, one out of every five washing machines sold in the United States was built by Maytag, and its products were so popular that it survived the Great Depression without posting a loss in any single year. By the 1970s, it had added dozens of product lines, from stoves to dishwashers, had began running television commercials featuring the now-iconic Maytag repairman, and had acquired several famous American names like Magic Chef and Hoover.

But fast-forward to 2004, and Maytag was hemorrhaging cash, its costs well above companies that had moved production outside the United States. Not helping matters was the fact that in spite of a sterling reputation for quality, its brand was considered passé in the wake of trendier lines from Viking and KitchenAid, not to mention stiff competition from General

Electric. The company went on the auction block, becoming the subject of a three-way bidding war between Ripplewood Holdings, a private investment group; Whirlpool Corporation; and a group that included Bain Capital, the Blackstone Group—and Haier.

But why, in 2004, would a company based in China, where demand for consumer goods was booming, be interested in acquiring an American brand—much less one that was past its prime? Michael Jemal, president of Haier America, thought that despite Maytag's troubles, the acquisition could hold possibilities for Haier, not least by helping to jump-start its efforts to raise visibility in the United States. "We do have ambitions, we want to achieve top-tier status," he said. "What better way to do that than by acquiring a company with significant platforms," meaning a broad product range. The two companies could then "combine our talents and manufacture at lower costs" and then, Jemal reasoned, win back a customer base with "better approaches in marketing than they had." But Haier's timing could not have been worse.

As it was bidding for Maytag, an uproar arose in Congress over an effort by the China National Offshore Oil Corporation, or CNOOC, to purchase Unocal, the venerable California oil producer whose gasoline was sold under the Union 76 brand. CNOOC's unsolicited bid, valued at $18.5 billion, raised serious objections from members of the House of Representatives (some of it at the urging of lobbyists from Chevron, who, not coincidentally, acquired Unocal in the end). The House voted to ask President Bush to review the deal's implications for national security, and the furor prompted CNOOC to withdraw its bid, but not before the controversy generated a huge firestorm of national attention—and no small amount of anti-Chinese sentiment.

Household appliances have little to do with national security, of course, but Jemal said Haier nonetheless felt the sting of the backlash. "Everybody was looking at it and thought we'd get caught in that storm," Jemal recalls. Throughout the country, the prospect of a Chinese company owning a legendary American brand caused a flurry of discomfort, with Jemal himself the target of anonymous critics on the Web, who took issue with an American who has thrown in his lot to help a company owned by China's Communist government. "Michael Jemal is one of the worst sort of slime there is," read one message posted on a Web site called Hall of Shame.

In the end, Haier caved to the pressure and backed out of the bidding, and the American behemoth Whirlpool bought Maytag for $21 a share, valuing the company at more than $1.7 billion (far more than Haier believed the company was worth). Since then, Whirlpool has shuttered Maytag's headquarters in Iowa and closed plants in Mississippi, Arkansas, and Illinois. While the Maytag name lives on, the majority of its employees have been let go, which Jemal believes would not have happened had Haier acquired the company.

But despite this setback, Haier continues to pursue American growth, although Jemal has no illusions that Haier will escape criticism as it expands. "Will we confront a political storm? We might," he admitted. The same could be said, really, for any foreign companies striving to compete against homegrown players.

Chapter Five

NOT IN WASHINGTON'S BACKYARD, EITHER

All is politics in this capital.

—THOMAS JEFFERSON

The sight was one that many diehard Democrats never thought they would witness: John Dingell, the powerful chairman of the House Energy and Commerce Committee and longtime champion of the Detroit auto companies, attending an event celebrating Toyota. But there he was, on a warm early autumn day in 2008, sitting in a front-row seat next to Michigan's governor, Jennifer M. Granholm. She had just given a warm, almost evangelical address welcoming hundreds of guests to the dedication of the new safety and engineering center in York Township, Michigan, and now it was Dingell's turn to address the crowd.

The room was quiet as Dingell lumbered up to the podium on crutches (following recent surgery), getting a gentle assist from Bruce Brownlee, the Toyota official who was the master of ceremonies. Though Dingell's frame was less imposing than in the days when he intimidated opponents on Capitol Hill, his voice was still the same.

"Good morning! This is a wonderful day!" he boomed across the audience of Toyota executives, local dignitaries, and the concert orchestra from a nearby high school. Choosing his words deliberately, Dingell expressed "thanks—gratitude—appreciation!" to the Japanese carmaker. "This is a magnificent facility, one which is going to help us work together to build a greater Michigan," he said. "I'm proud of what you do, and I will help see to it that you have success."

In attending the dedication, Dingell showed the careful line that Washington officials must tread when it comes to foreign investment. On one hand, lawmakers often face a need to proclaim their allegiance to the United States, everything from its flag to its sports teams to its corporations. On the other hand, they are bound to serve the best interest of their home states or congressional districts, whether by securing jobs for their constituents, charitable contributions for their communities, or capital that will jump-start economic growth.

No matter how much foreign companies may spend in the United States or how many millions of workers they employ, Washington is the place where the subject of investment from overseas touches the most nerves, the place where, in the end, nationalism always comes to the fore. As with most national debates, the fight over foreign investment is the loudest here. Sometimes the battle is all sound and no fury, but more often, it is existential for the companies that are involved.

For foreign companies hoping to do business in the United States, winning over the hearts and minds of the American public is only half the battle; in order to truly compete in the American marketplace, foreign investors need to win over the hearts and minds in Washington, as well. Of course, there are protectionist stirrings among lawmakers (especially those up for reelection) whenever American jobs are involved, but perhaps not surprisingly, opposition to foreign investment is never more apparent—or more vocal—in Washington than when national security issues are at stake. And there has been no better example of this in the past decade than the battle between Boeing and Airbus over the tanker contract from the United States Air Force.

THE TANKER BATTLE: BOEING VERSUS AIRBUS

The Farnborough International Airshow outside London is an aviation buff's dream. Held every other year, the show features the latest in commercial aircraft, jet fighters, private jets, and helicopters. Generals dressed in full regalia, their chests adorned with ribbons, stroll past corporate executives in expensive suits and sheikhs in white robes, as billions of dollars in deals are made in hospitality centers called chalets. Every afternoon during the weeklong show, Farnborough plays host to a two-hour flying display of jets, helicopters, and other aircraft, a spectacular showcase of all the companies' newest products. The visual display is so stunning and so loud that there is little choice but to find a good viewing stand and enjoy a catered lunch.

Given its audience, Farnborough is an ideal place for an aircraft manufacturer to capture attention. In July 2008, that's exactly what Airbus was looking for, with two of its most talked-about products. One was the mammoth A380 jet, capable of transporting five hundred people halfway around the world. And attention was what it got when Airbus's chief pilot put the jumbo jet through a series of maneuvers above the Farnborough runway that resembled the kind performed by Hollywood stunt pilots. To the astonishment of onlookers, the giant plane circled the field and dipped almost to the tarmac, then effortlessly floated back to the sky, making swift, graceful turns into the clouds above before emerging almost on its back. The audience broke into spontaneous applause as the A380 landed with barely more noise than a tiny Cessna.

Yet, despite this much-talked-about performance, it was the older A310, an all-white jet bearing the first version of the refueling equipment that helped Airbus win a $35 billion contract with the U.S. Air Force—which was now in question—that in the end, got the most attention.

While some units of EADS date back to the 1930s, the company's centerpiece, Airbus, was launched in 1970. It was very late to the airplane manufacturing game, entering the fray more than fifty years after William E. Boeing started the company that would eventually bear his name. When EADS, a consortium of three European companies—Germany's DaimlerChrysler Aerospace AG, Aerospatiale Matra of France, and Construcciones Aeronauticas SA of Spain—was initiated in 2000, it had no operations in the United States and employed only eleven people in a corporate office in Washington, D.C., mainly to represent the company to the German, French, and Spanish embassies there.

At the time, industry analysts expected EADS to concentrate on solidifying its role as Europe's leading defense contractor before branching out around the world. But EADS executives immediately recognized that in order to participate in two of the most important American industrial markets—defense and aviation—EADS would have to put down roots in America. "From the very beginning of the creation of EADS, we were looking at doing more in the United States in terms of production," said Mark Paganini, a French executive and the president of American Eurocopter, the company's civilian and military helicopter unit.

From the outset, EADS officials also knew that if they wanted to get contracts—either military or commercial—in the United States, they would have to overcome protectionist sentiment and win favor in Washington, and that the best way to do that would be to sell planes and equipment made in America, by Americans. "The U.S. market is the largest single market in the world in aerospace," said Paganini, who served on the team that created EADS and led its investor relations department as it prepared for its stock to be listed on global exchanges. "We wanted to sell in the U.S. and we wanted to be closer to the customer. Being in the U.S. would help us to sell here." Although EADS's primary focus for the United States was military equipment, EADS executives calculated that once it established a military foothold, the company could someday shift aircraft production entirely to the United States, posing a formidable challenge to Boeing on its home turf.

But the strategy was a bold gamble. American companies had a virtual lock on the $80 billion procurement budget allotted to the Pentagon, which makes up 47 percent of the world's military spending. A foreign company had never taken the front seat in a major American military program, although in the past some members of the consortium had participated as support companies to American contractors, providing technology and components in a secondary role. Beyond that, competition was fierce; Boeing, the formidable American jetmaker, had survived years of consolidation among airplane manufacturers to emerge as the only American producer of jet planes and was not about to let Airbus, which had already passed it in global aircraft sales, take away any more market share.

So it was no surprise that in March 2008, three months before the Farnborough exhibition, executives at Airbus's parent, EADS, were jubilant when Airbus, with its partner, the American military contractor Northrop Grumman, was chosen over Washington State–based Boeing for one of the biggest deals awarded by the Pentagon in years. Lucrative enough in itself, the initial phase of the contract was just a beginning; once the first 179 A330 planes were delivered, the contract was expected to expand to 500 planes, making its total value worth more than $100 billion. Eventually, the contract could open even more doors for Airbus to build planes in the United States market that Boeing so jealously guarded.

The Pentagon had awarded the contract to EADS based on five criteria, including the cost and price of the planes (Airbus's A330 versus the Boeing 767), past performance in fulfilling such contracts both in the United States and elsewhere, and the design of the aircraft (such as its takeoff performance, its fuel capacity, and its fuel economy once in flight). But even though some of the production work would be done at Airbus's main manufacturing center in Toulouse, France, the military officials stressed that one of the main reasons the contract was being awarded to EADS in partnership with Northrop Grumman was because the final assembly of the plane would take place at a new factory in Mobile, Alabama. This deal, the government said, would create twenty-five thousand jobs, and Alabama's lawmakers were crowing with excitement.

"Bringing these jobs to Alabama will solidify our stellar reputation as an industrial leader and send a strong message to the rest of the world: Alabama is open for business," said Alabama Republican Senator Richard Shelby. Meanwhile, Bob Riley, Alabama's governor, saw the investment by Airbus as the linchpin in the state's effort to sweep away its image as a economic and social backwater. "It's changing the whole dynamic of the state," said Riley, a Republican who is fond of wearing cowboy boots with his business suits. "It's redefining Alabama."

But the celebration was short-lived. Boeing, which had won and then lost an earlier contract to build the tanker planes amid a corporate scandal, vowed to fight its foreign competition with every political weapon in its arsenal. Over the next months, it did so, calling on its employees, unions, and sympathetic members of Congress, and appealing to the air force to overturn the decision. Finally, caving to political pressure from Boeing lobbyists, members of Congress (including House Speaker Nancy Pelosi, a California Democrat, who implied that Republican presidential candidate John McCain had interceded to make sure EADS got the work as payback to Boeing for a 2002 scandal), and others, the General Accounting Office reviewed the process through which the contract had been awarded and issued a report saying that errors had taken place in eight steps of the process.

As a result, the Pentagon decided to reevaluate the decision and announced in fall 2008 that it would restart the competition at a future date, even though the decision meant that the air force, whose refueling planes are on average twenty-five years old, would have to wait years for new jets. Thus, EADS saw its hard-fought victory slip away. And it may not be easy for them to win a second time, because Boeing has vowed to fight just as hard when the contract comes up again. "We intend to compete aggressively for this important program," Boeing's chief executive, W. James McNerney, Jr., said in late 2008.

The passionate and vocal outcry in Washington against awarding the military contract to foreign-owned EADS was about much more than protecting Boeing—it was about protecting the nation. Pundits, security experts, and lawmakers on both sides of the aisle questioned the wisdom of giving foreign nations (even our allies) unfettered access to military bases, engineering plans, and other classified information. "As far as I'm concerned, Northrop Grumman is a front for the French," declared David Hobson, at the time a Republican representative from Ohio.

"Choosing a French tanker over an American tanker doesn't make any sense to the American people, and it doesn't make any sense to me," added Todd Tiahrt, another Republican from Kansas, where Boeing has extensive operations. "If we were to compete for Air Force One today, it probably would go to a foreign manufacturer," Tiraht said in jest, according to National Public Radio. (All joking aside, he wasn't so far from the mark; EADS is likely to be among the companies vying to build the presidential fleet when the military next puts the contract up for bidding.)

In Seattle, where Boeing is a pillar in the community, the outcry against EADS was even more heated. "As a veteran, this really upsets me," said Lincoln Olson, a member of the International Association of Machinists and Aerospace Workers who was employed at Boeing's plant in Renton, Washington. "I'm going to email all my buddies from the army and tell them to email their congressmen." Ignoring EADS's plans to building a factory in Alabama, he said, "I'm going to let them know, 'Hey, we're not going to have a French-made product defending the United States.' " Added Clark Hailey, another Boeing worker, "This ain't going to fly with the American people. It's a slap in the face and I am not alone in this feeling."

While the contract with EADS did not violate any American trade or security regulations, the notion of giving other countries access to such vital military contracts was, for many people, more than unsettling. It didn't matter that Boeing, for years, had supplied military equipment to other governments around the world. That was simply an endorsement of an American company's strength—American Exceptionalism at its very finest. This was different, because it was us letting an outsider in, not the other way around.

For EADS, the outcome of the tanker battle signified more than just the loss of a lucrative contract, it signaled the loss of a six-year behind-the-scenes campaign to win over Washington— and with it, the American public at large. Back in 2002, when Ralph Crosby, a senior executive at Northrop Grumman, was recruited to join EADS as the head of its North American operations, he was given two weeks to come up with a North American strategy that would frame EADS's actions for years to come. He drafted a series of priorities, all with an eye toward assuaging the security concerns that many Americans felt toward EADS—and winning over Washington in the process. First, he consolidated all of EADS's operations in the United States under one umbrella, instead of having each business report to the company's individual business units overseas. This achieved two things: It made U.S. operations more transparent, and it transferred oversight and control from European officers to more trusted American ones. Crosby also decided to hire experienced managers with a background in American military and industrial contracts, in part so that EADS would not have to spend years developing relationships and in part to assure future contractors that EADS's managers had already been extensively vetted by the U.S. military.

EADS officials knew that if they wanted to win any battles in the halls of Congress, they'd have to overcome protectionist fears as well, and this meant they had to make a serious commitment to American production. This step was not only important to meet government requirements; it was critical if EADS was to be taken seriously by Congress and those wielding influence in key communities and states. "With commercial customers, the primary focus is on price, quality, and schedule. They don't care where it's built; they don't care where it's assembled or who provides it, as long as it's all legal," said Samuel Adcock, EADS's government affairs chief. "When you get into appropriated dollars, where it is built and where it gets spent becomes an operative issue."

Ultimately, none of these efforts were enough to quell the widespread national security concerns and overcome the kind of protectionist rhetoric that has always been aimed at foreign companies who challenge American icons—public opposition was simply too fierce. "There has probably never been as politically charged and politically divisive a contract evaluation and award than this one," said Adcock. "I've been in this town twenty-four years doing this and I've never seen anything like this."

A DIFFERENT OUTCOME FOR TATA

Tata has found itself at the center of a similar debate in Washington—but they were lucky enough to experience a different outcome. In 2005, alarm bells went off when the Tata subsidiary Videsh Sanchar Nigam Limited, or VSNL, paid $130 million for Tyco Global Network, which operated thousands of miles of undersea cable connecting North America, Europe, and Asia (beating out the American-owned Polaroid, which wanted to acquire Tyco Global but dropped out of the bidding). The transaction meant that an Indian company now owned the last piece of the undersea grid that channeled U.S. communications, giving the Indian government control over a significant portion of the world's submarine cable network, since India owned 25 percent of VSNL. And even though the Tyco Global deal won swift approval from the Treasury Department and other American agencies, including the Federal Communications Commission, which had granted VSNL a license to operate the portion that affected American communications, many lawmakers and pundits were demonstrably worried that it posed a national security threat. Senator Jon Kyl of Arizona, echoing the concerns of many on both sides of the aisle, claimed that VSNL had acted "in a fashion demonstrably hostile to U.S. military and commercial interests" (even though VSNL had pledged not to take any steps that would harm American security).

"There is something on its face that is troubling," Lou Dobbs, the CNN commentator, said on his program in May

2005. "The United States government is resting the national interest on, quote unquote, "promises" from a foreign company that is paying literally less than $200 million for an investment of three point—was it four billion dollars for this grid, with all of its implications for national security, its importance to national security communications. It's remarkable." But the rhetoric did not scuttle the arrangement, and in the years since, Dobbs's fears and those of others in Washington turned out to be for naught. There is no evidence that national security has been threatened by the sale to VSNL. "The system worked, the democracy worked, and yes, there were members of Congress involved, but the decision was the right one," Rosling said. For Tata the episode was part of its American learning curve, and they took it in stride. "We have had a brush with what can happen, but it worked out well."

INSIDER TURNED OUTSIDER, AND VICE VERSA

If it's Sunday it's *Meet the Press*, or so goes the NBC News slogan, and if it's *Meet the Press*, it's bound to be sponsored by Toyota. (Sometimes, the ads run right after those for Boeing.) The advertising campaign that Toyota has run for the past few years during the Sunday morning talk show was the brainchild of its group vice president for government affairs, Jo Cooper, who realized, soon after joining Toyota in 2005, that simply producing high-quality, fuel-efficient vehicles wasn't enough to win over the American public; that, like any brand that wants to gain share in a competitive market, Toyota would have to advertise. What's more, she realized that, unlike your average brand, her company was under heavy scrutiny from not just consumers but from Washington as well. So, to raise the company's profile and gain acceptance among a policy-minded audience, the corporate advertising strategy would have to tout Toyota's economic contributions and community efforts, rather than just its cars.

Like Sam Adcock and Ralph Crosby at EADS, Cooper is a veteran of national politics and no stranger to the workings of inside the beltway. She worked for former Senate majority leader Howard Baker, who later served as the U.S. ambassador to Japan, and Congressman Dick Cheney, who later became vice president, and had also spent time at the Environmental Protection Agency. Just before joining Toyota, she worked, albeit indirectly, for Detroit, as the executive director of the Alliance of Automobile Manufacturers, the primary trade group for car companies that build vehicles in the United States. Now she had to come up with a campaign that would assure viewers that Toyota was practically as American as a Detroit company.

In 2005, she launched a series of ads (part of Toyota's $900 million a year ad spending), strategically aired during public affairs talk shows, stressing Toyota's investments in communities nationwide. "Many members, while they might know we had a plant in their states, might not know the extent of investments in other states," Cooper said. Although the ads cost a pittance compared with the millions Toyota spends each year on advertising, the higher profile was a big change for Toyota. Until Cooper arrived, Toyota's Washington strategy was simply to monitor activities but never to play an activist role. The prevailing attitude was "Don't be too pushy, don't be too engaged, we're still visitors in this country, we're still respectful of the other companies, especially GM," Cooper said. But by 2005, with $15 billion already invested in the United States and more expansion expected, it became clear that a higher political profile was needed; there simply was too much at stake.

This is where Cooper came in. "We want you to take the Washington operation for Toyota and build it into what it needs to be" so that Toyota could be "a part of the deliberations for the auto industry," Dennis Cuneo, the senior executive then in charge of Toyota's legal and external affairs, told her. And build it she did.

By early 2007, Toyota listed $3.3 million in lobbying expenses and was assisted by seven outside firms. It had eight in-house lobbyists, Cooper included, and twenty-eight from outside firms. Unlike GM and many other American corporations, Toyota does not have a political action committee (to which employees donate money to be contributed to political candidates), nor does it contribute to individual candidates (its donations were split between the Republican and Democratic parties and their campaign committees), but one thing was clear: The company was no longer a political bystander. As GM's former vice chairman Robert Lutz declared, in a voice tinged with sarcasm, "I will tell you today—mind you, today—it is my considered opinion that Toyota has more clout in Washington than we do." He went on: "One of the sad things is, Toyota is so profitable and has plants in so many states that, frankly, they've got more congressmen and senators than General Motors does." And, when it comes to lobbying, "They outspend us." This was an exaggeration; lobbying data from OpenSecrets .org, the Web site run by the Center for Responsive Politics, showed that GM spent $6.4 million on lobbying in 2007 and had 109 registered lobbyists. But it couldn't be denied that, between its lobbying activity and its politically minded advertising campaign, Toyota's presence in Washington was being felt. "All we want is a fair hearing. Toyota just wants people to understand what our concerns are and who we are," Cooper said.

Toyota's attempts to use its newfound Washington clout ultimately backfired. In the spring of 2007, Toyota joined other carmakers in a vigorous campaign to fight legislation requiring higher fuel-economy standards, angering many in the environmental movement and alienating some of its closest allies. Until that point, the company's environmental credibility seemed bulletproof; its hybrid-electric Prius, beloved by environmentalists, was considered a shining example of what twenty-first-century companies could and should be doing to get consumers to change their gas-guzzling habits. But when the company flexed its muscles in Washington over the fuel-economy issue, even its most fervent supporters in the environmental movement felt sold out. "Their reputation as a green car company is absolutely inaccurate if not blatantly false," said Nick Magel, director of the Freedom from Oil Campaign run by the Global Exchange, an environmental activism group.

Even *New York Times* columnist Thomas Friedman, the longtime GM critic and Toyota supporter, now slapped the company. In a column entitled, "Et Tu, Toyota?" which was widely circulated in Detroit, he took aim at Toyota for fighting higher standards in a Senate version of the legislation. "Sad," Friedman wrote. "If Toyota were to take the lead on this front, it could enhance its own reputation and spur the whole U.S. auto industry to become more globally competitive. Hey, Toyota, if you are going to become the biggest U.S. automaker, could you at least bring to America your best practices—the ones that made you the world leader—instead of prolonging our worst practices? We have enough people helping us commit suicide."

Cooper was personally distressed by this backlash, and executives in Japan were worried about the mounting criticism of the company, especially at a time when Toyota's sterling image on quality had been shaken by a spike in recalls in Japan and in the United States. "A lot of our colleagues within the company were not happy," she admitted. However, Toyota did not leave the alliance nor did it distance itself from the group's effort to fight the fuel-economy legislation. The group eventually came around and supported a Senate version, passed into law, that raised fuel-economy standards to 35 mpg by 2020. But it was superceded in 2009 by President Obama's proposal to raise fuel economy even faster.

Still, the battle over fuel economy demonstrated Toyota's determination to weave itself into the fabric of the American economy, at no less than the highest political level; no matter how unpopular with the green movement, it showed that Toyota was ready to compete in the American political arena just like an American player. Cooper said she would continue to court favor and cultivate relationships with lawmakers who might be able to help advance Toyota's corporate interests, and she believes the company has never been better equipped to do so. "We're in such a stronger position now than we were [in previous decades]," she said. "We've got more plants, we've got more jobs, our dealer body is very strong, and we have suppliers who could engage on our behalf. We're much more an integrated part of the community in the U.S."

Cooper was confident that the tide of public opinion would eventually swing back in Toyota's favor, and she was right. Just eighteen months after the fuel-economy debate, when Detroit automakers came to Capitol Hill pleading for billions of dollars in federally backed loans, Toyota, once again the industry darling, found itself looking pretty good in comparison. As intense debate roiled Washington, and the Detroit companies were pummeled with criticism that they had failed to switch their model lineups swiftly enough to meet consumers' needs for fuel-efficient cars, politicians, pundits, and industry analysts cited Toyota as an example of what the Detroit companies should have done better. For once, few commentators or editorial writers pointed fingers at Japan, Germany, or any other country as the source of Detroit's woes.

In March 2009, the company found itself getting tacit support from the most important figure in Washington. President Obama pointed his finger squarely at the management of Detroit auto companies, not their foreign competition, when he deemed the restructuring plans submitted by GM and Chrysler to be "unviable" and forced GM's chief executive, Rick Wagoner, to step aside. As he talked about the recession that had gripped the industry, Obama said that even healthy companies—"like Toyota"—were having trouble dealing with the difficult economic conditions. It was clear that the president did not see Detroit's foreign competition as part of its problem.

"Despite the desires of some politicians to blame Toyota for some of the things that have happened in the U.S. auto industry, that's out of the mainstream," noted John Casesa, the auto industry analyst. "Americans don't blame Toyota or the Japanese for Detroit's problems anymore. They did, but now they think these are Detroit-specific problems." With Cooper as one of its generals, Toyota, he said, "has won the public relations war."

PROTECTIONISM BACKFIRES

As a nation, our feelings and attitudes toward foreign companies are undeniably complex. But over and over again, history has shown that however we might *feel* about foreign investment, protectionist policies aren't the answer—and can, in fact, have the opposite of their intended effects.

In the 1970s, when the Arab oil embargo and subsequent energy crisis caused supplies of gasoline to slow to a trickle and Detroit's gas guzzlers to fall out of favor, the Japanese companies, who built millions of small, fuel-efficient cars every year for their home market, had an ideal opening. American consumers soon flocked to the more economical Japanese vehicles, and by 1979 Japanese companies held 35 percent of the American market (a record that would hold for two decades, until oil prices reached record levels in 2008). As GM and Ford suffered deep losses and Chrysler lurched dangerously close to bankruptcy in the late 1970s, fearful Detroit executives and their political allies demanded that the American government act.

In 1981 the United States and Japan agreed to a voluntary restraint agreement limiting Japanese exports to the United States to 2.3 million vehicles a year. This meant that if the Japanese companies wanted to sell more, they had only one option: Produce those vehicles in American plants. Rather than fight the voluntary restraints, Japanese government officials decided to go along, for two reasons: They hoped it would ease political pressure on Japan to loosen its own restrictions on imports, and, quite simply, they didn't want to give up access to the world's most important car market.

The American government's justification for the deal was

that it offered a "level playing field," but what Detroit companies really hoped was that it would buy them time to outrun their Japanese rivals, said Professor Mira Wilkins at Florida International University. American executives thought, "All the Japanese need to do is invest in the United States and have the same level playing field and they'll discover how hard it is, and they won't be competitive at all," she said.

But over the next thirty years, the opposite took place. What was intended to hinder foreign companies' operations in the United States instead transformed them into their own American industry—"the new domestics," as Mississippi governor Haley Barbour calls them. In other words, what began as an effort to shore up Detroit instead helped hasten its demise. Workers in Detroit auto plants—the people the law was intended to protect—wound up the losers when the Big Three failed to adequately respond to the Japanese challenge, while workers in the American plants built by the companies from overseas turned out to be the ironic winners.

Protectionism can also backfire in other ways, causing friction between longtime friends. The perennial dispute between the United States and Canada over duties on softwood lumber has been one of the most significant disagreements between the two countries, which are each other's biggest trading partners. The dispute dates back to 1982, when American lumber interests first requested that the government place duties on imported Canadian lumber. They failed in several tries but in 2002, the Commerce Department placed tariffs on Canadian lumber.

When Canada protested, both the World Trade Organization and the board that oversees the North American Free

Trade Agreement ruled that imports of softwood did not harm the U.S. lumber industry. Meanwhile, the Canadian government said it would spend $20 million a year to pay the legal expenses of lumber companies, such as Abitibi-Consolidated and Weyerhaeuser, that wanted to fight the American move. Yet, the United States refused to back down on the duties, which had mounted to $5.3 billion by 2006. In response, Canadian lumber producers actually increased their shipments to the United States, figuring that economies of scale would help them overcome the added expense of sending lumber south of the border.

At the same time, a ready market for the Canadian lumber had emerged in areas of the United States that were hit by hurricane damage, such as Louisiana and Mississippi after Katrina. Even if the American government didn't want Canadian lumber, Americans themselves were understandably eager for it.

Finally, in 2006, a compromise was reached, and the United States agreed to refund about $4 billion of the money collected. By then, the debate had become emotional, entangling several Canadian prime ministers and Secretary of State Condoleezza Rice, not to mention a series of American and Canadian trade officials, and had soured an otherwise harmonious relationship between two nations who peacefully share a five-thousand-mile border. In Canadian eyes, "The lumber dispute has probably caused more harm than benefit to the United States," a report by the government of British Columbia concluded.

Sticky trade disputes aside, investing in America is often the best defense a foreign company can have against protectionism, for a simple reason. "It's harder to take a sledgehammer to a car from Alabama," Chris Briem, an economist with the University Center for Urban and Social Research at the University of Pittsburgh explained. No matter the president's sales talk, Alan Rosling at Tata predicts that the debate in Washington over foreign investment will inevitably shift, given the growing realization that the United States is part of a global economy. "I believe further down the track, the U.S. is going to come closer to where we are," said the British-born executive. "Even the U.S. can't hold back the tide of economic reality. I think the debate is likely over time to move more to where it is in the U.K., where it is not the nationality that is important, but instead people ask, 'Are you are a good investor or not? Are you the sort of company that's going to invest, and employ for the long term?' "

In the meantime, companies such as Toyota, EADS, Tata, and Haier are all drafting expansion plans in the United States, knowing that they cannot entirely escape protectionist sentiment—whether on Main Street or on K Street—but pushing on, nonetheless.

Chapter Six

FOREIGN OWNERS, AMERICAN MANAGEMENT

Managing is getting paid for home runs that some-one else hits.

—CASEY STENGEL

Barbara Roth, the chief executive of Eight O'Clock Coffee, has exactly the kind of résumé that marketing majors dream of. Roth, who has long dark hair and a wide smile, has worked for some of the biggest names—and helped them create some of the more delicious products—in the consumer world. At Kraft Foods, she was in charge of the Polly-O lineup of dairy items, which includes string cheese, that portable pull-apart snack that mothers often hand their small children after a busy afternoon at preschool.

After leaving Kraft, she went to the Leaf Candy Company, the maker of Heath bars, Whoppers malted milk balls, and the spearmint jelly candies that gave the company its name, and eventually wound up at the Hershey Company, which acquired Leaf. But after having spent years marketing candy products, she was not eager to hang around Hershey—it was time for something new. So in 2002, she moved on to a category that piqued her interest: beverages.

Roth wanted to learn the business literally from the ground up, so she joined a small company in Hawaii that owned a coffee plantation and grew four different types of beans. There, Roth learned about every step of coffee growing, from harvesting the raw green coffee beans to all the myriad ways of roasting and grinding them. For someone used to working for major corporations, the work offered a break from the gray winter skies of the mainland but was also enormously challenging. Eventually, its owners directed her to shut the business down, because high labor costs made it unprofitable. But like a five-cup a day addict, she was hooked; coffee was now in her blood.

So Roth joined Eight O'Clock Coffee, which had been spun off by A&P. Her first job was to find a buyer for the company. She found one in Gryphon, an investment group, and kept Roth in place to turn Eight O'Clock around and make it attractive to buyers. And that's exactly what she did. When the brand came on the market again in 2005, India's Tata Group was ready to pounce.

Tata had been looking for a top-notch American coffee brand to add to its growing beverage group that already included Tetley Tea, which Tata purchased in 2000. But such prominent names rarely come on the market. "There are not that many acquisitions that come up in the coffee space that have relative strength across the U.S.," Roth said. Also, Tata might have been a major player in India, but it did not have a strong background in or understanding of the United States market—and its managers were willing to admit that.

This is why Tata has given Roth and other American managers the authority to run their operations as they set fit. "They don't have the attitude that they know this marketplace and this business better than we do. They figure we know what we're doing and that's why they bought us," said Roth.

Roth's transformation of Eight O'Clock coffee was so successful that when it went up for sale, Gryphon had a choice of about ten bidders, including some major American names, Roth said. Despite Tata's foreign origins, the investors found their offer the most appealing. "They understood the vision, they understood what was going on, and they were ready to take it to a different phase and place of our lives," Roth said. Tata assured her that Eight O'Clock would remain a stand-alone business, which was not something that other companies could guarantee. "If it had been bought by Kraft or Proctor, the whole business would be folded into one of their existing operations," Roth said. "As a foreign-based company, they didn't have things to fold it into. It aligned us in a complementary way" with the rest of Tata.

Careerwise, Tata's hands-off approach has worked in Roth's favor. For nearly three years now, she has had the opportunity to shape Tata's beverage portfolio, helping the company turn its collection of different brands scattered around the world into a more cohesive family of offerings. In fact, the work she is doing mirrors everything that is going on at the top of Tata under Alan Riding, the company's head of globalization.

One step that she has already taken is introducing a gourmet brand of coffee under the Good Earth label, which already included a line of herbal teas (readers of *Real Simple* and *Bon Appetit* magazines have become accustomed to ads for Good Earth coffee, made from 100 percent arabica beans, which Tata markets as a slightly less expensive alternative to brands like Starbucks and Peet's). Her future goals may include introducing American consumers to the variety of products that Tata sells in markets overseas, such as Mount Everest Mineral Water, sold by the company throughout southern Asia. Roth thinks the name alone might capture the attention of sports-minded consumers. But she doesn't feel under pressure to overreach; even modest progress in the American market can benefit Tata internationally, simply because the United States offers so much potential.

"The U.S. is a huge, huge country. Sometimes I didn't appreciate how large the U.S. is and what it contributes around the world," said Roth, who grew up in Scarsdale, New York, and holds degrees from the University of Vermont and Northwestern. "You're seeing from the financial crisis how much it impacts the rest of the world, in a positive and negative way. We are big. We might not be in growth mode, like Brazil or China or Russia. But if you can carve even a small share out, that represents a significant business on a global level."

Roth spoke on the same day that her boss, Ratan Tata, was in New York, where he was meeting with some of his American business heads, and being honored by the British-American Business Council. Although Roth was suffering from a bad cold, she was determined to make the trip across the Hudson River from her headquarters in Montvale, New Jersey, and spend some time in meetings. "I really haven't had the opportunity to see the things that go on around Mr. Tata," and the chance was too good to pass up, sniffles or no sniffles, she confided. After all, Tata had traversed waterways far vaster than the Hudson to watch Roth and others in action.

THE HOLY GRAIL

For many managers, the holy grail in American business has arguably always been the corner office. Indeed, the possibility, however remote, of attaining that corner office—and all the success it signifies—has been enough to motivate generations of managers in businesses small and large. Some make it; many don't. Nonetheless, most press on because at the core of our American work ethic is the assumption that anyone with enough brains, talent, and connections can make it to the top.

But at foreign-owned companies, this is not necessarily the case. Many are still controlled by founding families, where successive generations of CEOs are descended from a founding patriarch. Toyota, for example, is again run by a member of the Toyoda family, after more than a decade of outside managers, and the Tata family of India has been in charge of all of its holdings since the day the company was founded. Even in foreign companies that are run by outsiders, the possibility of an American manager making it to the top can seem remote. For some American managers lusting after that American Dream of the corner office, the excuse for refusing to explore a career at an overseas-based firm is simple: "You'll never be able to run the place."

But this excuse is a weak one; in today's global economy, the concept of a native-born chief executive is changing. For example, Howard Stringer, who is British, rose to run Sony of Japan, while Carlos Ghosn, born in Brazil to Lebanese parents, runs Nissan of Japan and Renault of France, and Sergio Marchionne, a Canadian Italian, runs Fiat.

Even at foreign companies that have yet to yield control to

executives born in other countries, there is still a significant opportunity for Americans to wield power. Americans can run global operating units, American divisions, and individual plants. Americans serve as managing directors, vice presidents, or board members. What's more, experience at a foreign company can be a stepping-stone to a top job at an American one. In 2007, two executives in Toyota's American operations—James Press, the highest-ranking American in the company, and James Farley, a vice president at Toyota Motor Sales—returned to Detroit, where each had started his career. Press became copresident of Chrysler, and Farley the president of Ford.

For executives who do decide to stay at foreign firms, even if the path to the corner office isn't exactly straight and narrow, the journey can be rewarding. Foreign companies can offer American mangers just as many, if not more, opportunities for career advancement, learning, and professional growth, as do American ones.

FIVE-STAR OPPORTUNITIES

Raymond Bickson has been involved in the hospitality business since junior high school, when his father, Irwin Bickson, one of the founders of Budget Rent A Car, moved the family from Chicago to Hawaii, where he ran the company's popular franchises at airports and hotels across the islands (and became so popular himself, in fact, that Irwin was known in Honolulu as "the mayor of Waikiki"). From eighth grade until after his high school graduation, Raymond "washed cars, rented cars, all that" as part of his role in the family business, recalled, the younger Bickson (whose brother attended classes with Barack Obama).

But the rental car business was "not sexy" to him, so Bickson, who had watched Honolulu grow into an international tourist destination, instead chose to pursue a hotel career, attending Cornell University and training in Berlin and in Lausanne, Switzerland. He spent ten years with Regent Hotels, fifteen years with Raphael Hotels, and became general manager of the Mark, a luxury hotel on East Seventy-seventh Street, near New York's Central Park.

Bickson, like all good hotel managers, kept track of the preferences of his most important guests, including, albeit unknowingly, Ratan Tata, who stayed at the Mark during trips to the United States. All Bickson knew about Tata was that he was an important business magnate from India, so it came as a surprise when Tata summoned him to his suite one day and offered him a job as the number two executive with Indian Hotels, one of the oldest companies in the Tata empire. "I didn't even know he had hotels in his portfolio," Bickson said.

Bickson came to Indian Hotels at what turned out to be a precipitous time. In the years since the Indian government had loosened rules regulating foreign investment, thirty-seven new hotel brands had opened properties across India, hoping to capitalize on the rapid growth in the country's high-tech, finance, entertainment, and telemarketing businesses. With Tata's hotel group facing more competition from around the world, Bickson concluded that Indian Hotels would have to grow internationally in order to stay in the game. He looked at twenty-five destinations around the world and decided that a key focus would be the United States.

"If one really wants to be global, you have to be present in the U.S. market, because it is such an important market in the travel and tourism industry," he said. His first ambitious efforts landed Indian two of the country's best-known hotels, the Pierre in New York and the Ritz-Carlton in Boston.

Opened in 1930, the Pierre sits at the corner of Sixtieth Street and Fifth Avenue in New York, kitty-corner from the Plaza and just up the street from such shopping landmarks as Bergdorf Goodman and Saks Fifth Avenue. Owned for a time by J. Paul Getty, the Pierre featured both a hotel and seventy-five cooperative apartments, whose residents included Elizabeth Taylor, Yves Saint Laurent, and Sumner Redstone, the owner of Viacom. At the time, the hotel was managed by Four Seasons Hotels and Resorts, the Canadian group headed by Isadore Sharp. But Four Seasons had opened a new hotel a few blocks from the Pierre, and Sharp saw no need for two New York properties. So he and Bickson struck a deal, and in 2005 Indian Hotels took over the lease. Soon after, Indian began a major renovation, costing $700,000 a room (completed in 2009).

By then, Bickson also had acquired several five-star hotels in Boston and San Francisco, and was seeking out opportunities in Chicago, Los Angeles, Miami, and Washington, D.C. The chance to acquire such well-known hotels is rare, and Bickson, who is in charge of twenty-two thousand employees and runs a group that produces $41.5 billion in revenue, is relishing his responsibilities. He doesn't have any sense that his opportunities are limited by the fact that he is at a foreign-owned, family-run company.

For Bickson, though, there has been bitter with the sweet. In December 2008, he was trapped in his Mumbai office for thirty-six hours during the terrorist attacks that centered on a series of hotels, including the Taj, Indian Hotels' flagship property. More than 150 people were killed and the Taj suffered significant damage. The hotel reopened two weeks later, with greater security.

This horrible tragedy has, if anything, only reinvigorated Bickson in his primary ambition—to make the Taj brand the Indian equivalent of the world's best-known luxury hotel chains. "I came in here to run the luxury hotels, I didn't come to be CEO," he said. "It's the experience of a lifetime."

THE TOYOTA CLASSROOM

For some executives, like Raymond Bickson, a position at a foreign company is a unique opportunity to jump in, take the reins, and fulfill one's professional aspirations. For others, the learning curve is a bit steeper. Such was the case for Norm Bafunno, for whom a managerial job at Toyota has been an ongoing education—and an invaluable one at that.

On a cold and gray December day in 2007, Bafunno was deep into one of the most difficult tasks any manufacturing manager faces: starting production for a new model. Bafunno was on day ten of the launch for the Toyota Sequoia, a big sport-utility vehicle then built at Toyota's plant in Princeton, Indiana. He should have been a nervous wreck, as dozens of problems often crop up during those early stages of production, and stress levels are often through the roof. But Bafunno, then the senior vice president of manufacturing, production, and quality planning control at Princeton, was relaxed as he sat chatting in a company conference room. After ten years at Toyota, which he joined after a fourteen-year stint at General Motors, he had survived plenty of product launches.

At an American company, his quarter century of experience would have qualified him for that coveted corner office, but in Toyota terms, said Bafunno, "I'm a rookie." To be sure, Toyota considered him a valuable player, and in 2009, he was promoted to vice president of production engineering for the company's North American manufacturing operations, giving him responsibilities at a collection of plants. For Bafunno, the chance for a fresh start was the most appealing part of the job. By the time he left GM in 1997, his old company was better known for shutting plants than for opening new ones, and the idea of joining a plant in its infancy was too good to pass up, he said. Plus, Toyota would be an education, and a chance to "grow in responsibility," he reasoned.

Upon arriving in Indiana, however, Bafunno experienced an awakening. In American companies, "the first thing people want to talk about is the best achievements," he said. So, armed with his résumé from GM, he was ready to share what had worked and what he had accomplished, at the Pontiac plant where he had most recently served as an assistant manager. But his new colleagues at Toyota, he soon learned, were not impressed. Heavily influenced by the mores and values of Japanese culture, Toyota's focus was not on individual achievements or on taking time to congratulate managers for what was going right. Instead, the company wanted managers to examine what was going *wrong* and find methods to improve, a practice called *kaizen*. Unlike American companies, who reward managers for excelling, Toyota deliberately puts its managers in situations where they do not already have the skills to perform, said Jeffrey Liker, the University of Michigan professor. The process of learning is just as much a part of a manager's job as directing other employees, Liker said. At first, Bafunno found the adjustment uncomfortable. "It's not inherent, it's not human nature," Bafunno said. "People think, I'm a negative person if I bring this up. But really, the manager, or the general manager or the team leader, everybody is there to support each other."

Bafunno soon found a mentor in Seizo Okamoto, the executive who had been sent from Japan to open the Princeton factory. Mentoring is a common practice at the company (and, in fact, in Japanese culture itself), where senior managers are expected to share what they have learned with younger supervisors, thus passing along the company's values and practices. Even Toyota's chairman, Fujio Cho, has taught hundreds of classes in the Toyota Production System, which he learned from his own mentor, Taiichi Ohno, the creator of TPS.

At Princeton, Okamoto and Bafunno, the veteran Japanese executive and the young American plant manager, spent hours in discussions that ranged from the practical to the philosophical. Okamoto was not there to dictate instructions to Bafunno: Like a professor teaching in the Socratic method, he was there to ask questions in order to find the solutions, Liker said. Bafunno was used to an entirely different GM culture in which information was power, to be held close to the vest and rarely shared with underlings. GM managers were conditioned to dole out what they knew only when necessary, all the time striving to wangle information out of others equally reluctant to share.

In contrast, "part of the approach at Toyota is to share information and the process about how things are done," Bafunno explained. But at the same time, the company places an emphasis on encouraging newcomers to reach their own conclusions. Okamoto "would spend a lot of time not giving answers, but talking about, 'Here's what I see and here's what you see,' " Bafunno said. Rather than correct him, the elder executive would ask, "Have you thought about this more?" Years later, Bafunno realized that his mentor's goal was "for me to investigate" rather than be spoon-fed the right answers.

Okamoto also taught Bafunno a fundamental Toyota philosophy, *genchi genbutsu*, meaning "go to the spot" or see things with your own eyes. And when he did "go to the spot" in the Princeton plant, Bafunno often discovered not only problems that needed to be solved but also people who needed guidance, just the way Okamoto was instructing him. When the plant opened, many Princeton employees, called team members, were entirely new to building cars. Like Amy Lindsey, the former Estée Lauder manager we met in the introduction, these workers were hired for their potential, not their automotive expertise. So it was up to managers like Bafunno to teach them the ways of Toyota's legendary production system—lessons they could then pass on to their current and future peers, just as Okamoto had done for him.

In that assignment, Bafunno sat down twice a week with plant employees for lunch and learn sessions—the learning mainly on his part, he says. "We eat a sandwich together, and people ask me anything. 'Are we getting a new product? Is Toyota expanding? Is Toyota doing good or bad? How's our quality?' " At Princeton, as at Toyota's other factories, workers continually offer ideas ranging from the simple to the complex, from improving the ergonomics of a manufacturing process to smoothing out bottlenecks on the assembly line. Time is devoted every day to going through the suggestions, which are put in place quickly, sometimes on the very next shift. While this emphasis on mentorship, problem solving, and a two-way exchange of ideas may not seem revolutionary, it was something that was woefully lacking in many American companies—that is, until popularized by Toyota.

Soon after Toyota opened its first factories in America and began implementing TPS at its U.S. locations, American managers and executives realized that the Japanese company was on to something valuable. Impressed by the company's efficient operations, lucid business philosophies, and consistent product quality, every business leader wanted a page out of Toyota's playbook. Companies such as Chrysler, UPS, and even hospitals embraced TPS as the solution to their problems. Thus, a management fad—one that would enlighten countless managers and transform businesses across the country—was born.

"DIRT SEEDS"

The education to be gained at a foreign company isn't extended to just executives and high-level managers; there is much a foreign company can teach the average worker as well. For Brian Howard, the Toyota worker we met in Chapter 2, a job at a Japanese company has been a cultural education as well as a professional one.

In September 2002, exactly a year after the terrorist attacks in New York and Washington, Howard traveled to Japan to visit Toyota's manufacturing headquarters. Prior to the trip, Howard hung a map on the wall in his son's room, with a dot on Nagoya, near Toyota's offices in Toyota City, where he planned to stay. When he came back, he eagerly shared with his son all that he had learned about Japan, including a few words in Japanese and all kinds of interesting customs. For example, he learned he didn't have to bow to his Japanese hosts (as he'd believed); it was all right to exchange a firm handshake instead. He was also pleased to learn that it was okay to skip the whale sushi at the welcoming dinner, since the Japanese did, too. "We were watching them and said, 'If they aren't eating it, we aren't eating it," Howard said with a laugh.

But much of the trip was spent visiting and studying Toyota factories, including the Tsutsumi plant in Toyota City that acts as a sister factory to the Georgetown, Kentucky, complex. He observed how his Japanese counterparts operated the assembly line, and he brought back a number of valuable ideas to test out back home, where Howard supervises a group of twenty-two team members, or assembly line workers, in the factory paint shop. In any factory—whether it makes automobiles or ceramics or toy trains—the paint shop is one of the most crucial areas, since consumers are often quick to judge the quality of a product by the quality of its paint job. So Howard's job at Georgetown, to oversee the application of topcoat to the painted car bodies, is an important one.

Each morning, he dons a lint-free paint smock, or a set of coveralls, much like a painter's jumpsuit, along with steel-toed boots and a pair of safety goggles. He arrives at the plant before 6 a.m. and performs a series of tasks to make sure that the equipment is ready to roll. This includes launching a "dummy spray," which tests the process to make sure the nozzles and other equipment are free of debris, such as lint and hair, that can easily spoil the painted surface of a car.

Once the equipment is ready, Howard pushes a button and the cars begin rolling through a giant painting booth, the size of a football field, one car every ninety-five seconds. As they exit, each one is dusted off by a roll of big ostrich feather dusters, as though in a giant car wash, while gusts of ionized air are blown onto the cars. This vacuums off any dust before the cars receive their final coat, Howard explained. Throughout the process, Howard is constantly on the lookout for "dirt seeds," those specs of dirt that might seem too small to matter but can ruin an entire paint job. "Basically, our biggest enemy in the paint department is dirt seeds. So the quickest way, and the best way, to improve quality in a paint shop is to minimize dirt levels," Howard said.

His best ideas for doing so came from his visit to Toyota's factories in Japan, where workers are even more vigilant in their battle against dirt. "They were very, very good in controlling seeds," Howard said, with admiration. One method they used was to hang sheets of sticky plastic material that the American visitors nicknamed "bug netting" inside the booth to catch the dust particles that were floating in the air. To assist the effort, they would spray a very fine water mist, high up against the ceiling, which settled the flying dust in the air, allowing it to fall against the bug netting.

It took a little over a year after he returned from Japan, but Howard eventually convinced the Georgetown plant to install both the mist sprayers and the bug netting inside the paint shop. Borrowing another idea from overseas, he added another ingenious step; there is now a pipe attached to the bug netting that collects the water spray, sends it to be filtered, and recirculates it to be used again. "The dirt particles land in the water, they're filtered out, and the water comes back around," he explained.

Another thing Howard brought back from his trip to Japan—which proved even more useful than whether to eat whale sushi and how to catch dirt seeds—was a new and improved outlook on how to manage his team and run his assembly line. In Japan, whether on a factory floor or in an executive boardroom, business is conducted in a calm, thoughtful manner, and the focus is on solving problems, continuous improvement, and collaborative effort. Howard brought that spirit back with him and, there is little racing about in his area on the factory floor. The employees move at a regular pace, and team leaders talk to team members in measured tones, if sometimes raised above the din of the assembly line. "There's not a whole lot of urgency, as long as everything is running smoothly. Small problems are common, little things that you deal with on a daily basis like a spray gun that starts spitting all over, and you have to change that out, that's fairly routine," he said.

"Big problems, if you see this thing's broken, we're going to be down for an hour, you start to see people really hustling," he said. Workers ask themselves, "What do we need to do?" and when a solution is reached, everyone works together to execute it. Howard smiled. "It creates a little chaos, but it's controlled chaos."

Group leaders like Howard are routinely promoted by Toyota to administrative jobs within its manufacturing operations. Howard has taken the classes necessary to apply but has not done so, although he is glad to know the opportunity exists. While he hasn't moved up as high as he once expected, the responsibilities of a team leader have satisfied his ambitions. "I'm content where I'm at, I guess you'd say; I haven't pursued advancement. But it's there if I wanted," he said.

For many Americans who live in a culture that so values individual achievement and personal advancement (that is, the corner office), embracing the foreign ways of doing business can be a challenge. As a result, foreign companies will need to keep Americans' competitive nature in mind and find a balance that offers potential for both fulfillment and learning, as they recruit executives and managers in years to come. That balance will go along way toward selling Americans on the idea of managing foreign companies—and it will also help sell foreign companies on the value of American managers. All that is key to the future of our economy, because American workers, companies, and, in fact, American society in general, have much to learn from our foreign counterparts.

THE AMERICAN MARKETPLACE

Foreign companies are a boon to the American marketplace for the jobs they create, the capital they infuse, the skills they teach, and the opportunities they afford managers, workers, and executives alike. But that's not all. By spurring competition, fostering innovation, introducing new technologies, and creating newer, better, and even cheaper products, foreign companies are also exerting a powerful and positive impact not only on the careers of employees and managers, but also on the American marketplace as a whole.

While critics of free trade would contend that allowing the sale of foreign-made products drives up consumer prices and creates unnecessary competition for American businesses, in reality this is often not the case; in fact, many of the goods produced by foreign-owned companies do not directly compete with goods produced by American companies but rather complement them. If it wasn't for the vast array of products sold in American stores—from clothing to electronics, and from commuter jets to kitchen stoves—that come only from foreign manufacturers, American consumers would lose much of the choice and variety in the marketplace that they have come to expect and enjoy, according to Donald Grimes, the University of Michigan economist. The United States simply does not have the ability to replace them in any kind of orderly fashion. What's more, if foreign companies could not sell their products here, the only alternative for the United States economy would be to focus entirely inward—a daunting prospect given a trade deficit that stood at $40.3 billion in early 2008.

Even when products made by companies based overseas do compete, this competition keeps American companies on their toes, which is good for the health of the economy as a whole. "We are never going to be able, realistically, to fix ourselves by walling ourselves off," said Joe Nocera, a business columnist at the *New York Times*. "That breeds inefficiency and higher prices, and creates trade wars. Besides, we [as a country] can *learn* from others coming to our shores." And, this education comes in many forms—not just in production systems and management styles, but in new ideas, innovations, and inroads into the global marketplace.

IMPORTING FOREIGN INNOVATION

Most foreign companies who have come to the United States have brought new ways of doing business with them. These methods have been both organizational, like the way Toyota runs its factories, or technological, like the way Sony designs its state-of-the-art digital storage devices. In fact, Japanese companies such as Toyota, Nissan, and Sony have long set the pace, and are still doing so, for innovation in everything from automotive production to personal audio player design, to clean energy technologies. As these new methods and technologies arrive on our shores, they are often adopted and implemented at many American offices, plants, and factories, which in turn improves production efficiency, enhances product quality, and spurs further innovation at our homegrown companies.

In 1998, Nissan revolutionized assembly line production in the United States when it pioneered and introduced its new IBAS—intelligent body assembly system—to the manufacturing world. Prior to its implementation, factories had to be torn up and machinery replaced every time the line changed over to a new model (as American factories had been doing since the early twentieth century). But with the IBAS system, which was installed at Nissan's factory in Smyrna, Tennessee, any model could be built on any one line—all Nissan had to do was reprogram computers and robots so that the machinery took into account the changes in the car or truck. In other words, the adjustments were made in software, not in hardware, which increased output because it allowed for much faster and more efficient transition between models.

The IBAS system helped the Smyrna plant repeatedly win

the top ranking on the manufacturing efficiency studies conducted by Harbour and Associates and was one of the main reasons that American manufacturers, from car companies to auto parts suppliers, who had once been the world's standard for manufacturing expertise, flocked to Tennessee to learn Nissan's secrets.

Similarly, Toyota brought an innovative new manufacturing technology to the American marketplace in 2004, when it introduced its global body line (GBL) to the manufacturing complex in its Georgetown, Kentucky, plant. I first saw the system on a visit to Japan in 2002, and it was later introduced in Toyota's plant in Valenciennes, France. Previously, each vehicle was clamped together on pallets—big pieces of tooling that held the car together so it could be welded—that varied according to the size of the car, which meant that Toyota had to change pallets for each type of vehicle it built. It was an inefficient, time-consuming, expensive system.

But with the GBL, the car underbodies simply flow into a main welding area, where about six hundred robots, which perform the welding, are sent signals that tell them which kind of vehicle they will be working on. The car body slides into place, while the robots move into the location they will need to be in to perform the welding. It's a tight fit, so Toyota mapped out the welding choreography on computer screens long before it installed the robots. But since there's no need for the big pallets, or for changing the equipment for each new model, the process moves more smoothly and takes up half the space it used to. This, in turn, cuts down on the time, labor, and cost of producing each model—a boon to consumers as well as to the company's bottom line, since it allowed Toyota to charge less for higher quality vehicles.

Both Nissan's idea and the one implemented at Toyota were inspirations for General Motors, which made an extensive push this decade to transform its factories into flexible plants; GM even boasted that once it was finished with its work, its plants would be even more efficient than Toyota's. The first fruits of GM's efforts showed up in its Delta Township, Michigan, plant, which opened outside Lansing in 2006. Thanks to its own flexible body system, similar to the ones at the Japanese companies, the plant could now build a greater variety of Saturn, Buick, GMC, and Chevrolet models faster and more efficiently. Unfortunately, the plant was barely open for two years before a deep slump in sales forced GM to eliminate one shift of workers there, and cut production, so the full impact of what Nissan and Toyota inspired has yet to be seen.

NET, NET, NET

Few executives, either at foreign companies or American ones, have a freezer named after them. But Michael Jemal, the chief executive of Haier America, can claim that distinction. During a meeting with Haier product managers a few years ago, Jemal scribbled down a novel idea for a chest-style freezer with a pull-out drawer, so that owners wouldn't have to dive deep to retrieve cuts of meat or cartons of ice cream. The company's engineers came up with a prototype in seventeen hours, and the "Michael Freezer," as it is known in China, is sold by Haier around the world.

The freezer episode typified how quickly Haier, the world's fourth largest dry goods company, can turn around an innovative new product idea. In fact, the whole story of Haier's trajectory in America typifies the impact an innovative, forward-thinking foreign company can have on the American marketplace.

Built in 1924, the fifty-two-thousand-square-foot stone building at the corner of West Thirty-sixth Street and Broadway previously served as headquarters for the Greenwich Savings Bank. Today, above a row of columns that are illuminated in blue at night, a tall series of brass letters announces THE HAIER BUILDING while an American flag flutters below. "This building is a fixture of New York City. It helps people understand that Haier America is an American company," explained James Liess, a spokesman for Haier America. "By being in this building, Haier secured a local footprint in the city and the country."

Ten-foot-tall brass doors open into a nearly ten-thousand-square-foot rotunda that used to be the heart of the Greenwich Savings Bank but has since been converted into a ballroom where Haier America hosts new product introductions and showcases its products for appliance buyers and the home goods media. Inside the elevator that takes visitors to the company's basement offices, a television set constantly plays Haier's latest television commercial, set to its theme song, "Take Me Higher!" A glass door opens to a modest lobby, where the Haier logo is mounted on a plaster wall behind the reception desk. Here, there is another American flag, as well as a less-familiar flag, red with one large gold star and four small ones—the flag of China.

Haier's roots date to the 1920s, when its forerunner began as a refrigerator company in Qingdao, on China's northeastern coast. After the establishment of the Peoples' Republic of China in 1949, the refrigerator maker became a state-owned company but drifted for years, turning out substandard products at a snail's pace. In 1984, the modern version of Haier, called the Qingdao Refrigerator Company, was launched as a joint venture with a German firm, the Liebherr Group. Zhang Ruimin, a factory manager who had studied Western management theories and production techniques, was put in charge.

In 1992, the company decided to take on a Western-sounding name. It borrowed from the last two syllables of its German partner, whose name was pronounced "lee-bow-higher" to become the Qingdao Haier Group and eventually just the Haier Group. By the 1990s, the Haier Group had diversified beyond refrigerators to microwave ovens, air conditioners, and freezers and expanded to international markets such as Indonesia, the Philippines, and Malaysia, but there was only one big market where Zhang still wanted to be: the United States.

In 1994, American-born Michael Jemal was running a small Brooklyn-based chain of music and electronics stores called Discount House of Sounds. When Welbilt, his refrigerator supplier, ran into financial problems, Jemal, seeing a unique opportunity where others might have only looked for a new supplier, gathered several investors together and bought Welbilt.

A few months later, Jemal traveled to China seeking manufacturers to provide products he could sell under the Welbilt name. He spotted a billboard for Haier and drove to the company's headquarters. Pretty soon, he'd struck a deal for Welbilt to become Haier's distributor in the United States. But he had bigger plans than simply putting the Welbilt name on Haier's products. He wanted to do what was more or less unthinkable at the time: start an American branch of a Chinese manufacturer.

For years, Jemal, a student of the American automobile industry, had watched foreign car manufacturers expand in the United States. "We all saw it happen with the Japanese in the eighties, and the Koreans in the nineties," he recalls, and he didn't see why an appliance maker couldn't follow the same path, as long as he could sink roots into the country, rather than simply be an exporter. "We saw a very big potential for a Chinese company to come here," he said. "If they demonstrated a different business model—come here, localize, and invest here—they stood a chance to succeed in the long run."

He admits that his plan seemed counterintuitive, particularly in the 1990s, when China's cheap sources of labor and fast production processes made it a far more attractive place to do business than the United States. Why would a Chinese company, with a huge home market, low costs, and endless opportunity in southern Asia, want to make the leap across the Pacific? One explanation lay in China's push to be seen as a global economic power. "The U.S. is a very tough market," said Bradley Farnsworth, director of the Center for International Business Education at the University of Michigan's Ross School of Business. "The thing is, if you're a CEO of a company in a developing country, the U.S. is sort of the ultimate test. It establishes you as a true multinational."

So Jemal figured that if he could tap an underserved corner of the U.S. market with Haier products from China, he could eventually convince the company to take the manufacturing plunge in America. Jemal found that underserved market in small refrigerators (the kind that college students buy for their dorms), wine refrigerators, and chest freezers, like the kind that would eventually bear his name.

Haier gave him a $100,000 advertising budget—peanuts for a brand trying to establish itself nationally—so Jemal had to spend the money strategically. Inspired by a road sign that had caught his eye on a trip to China, he bought billboards in Bentonville, Arkansas, near the corporate headquarters of Walmart, and in Minneapolis, next to the offices of Target. His clever strategy worked; soon, Haier's biggest customers included Walmart, which bought hundreds of thousands of refrigerators and air conditioners annually, and Target, which frequently featured Haier's fridges in its back-to-school advertising circulars.

By then, Haier decided the time was right for an American factory. In 1999, South Carolina's governor, Jim Hodges, stood next to China's ambassador to the United States, Li Zhaoxing, at the ground-breaking ceremony for Haier's first American manufacturing plant in Camden, South Carolina. By 2002, the plant, with its two hundred employees, was up and running, and earning Haier revenue of $200 million a year in the United States. The start was difficult. "We took a major hit getting it up and running," Jemal acknowledged. But he refused to give up. "Even though it did not make economic sense from the get-go, we thought that by sticking to the strategy, employing American workers, and building products specifically for the American market, we would start there."

Wisely, Jemal decided that U.S. operations should concentrate its efforts on the products that were most popular among Americans: compact refrigerators, chest freezers, and wine refrigerators (very popular at a time when Americans were learning more about vintages and collecting fine wines). These all sold well because they were well-priced, high-quality, and, most important, built with an eye toward satisfying the changing tastes and needs of the American consumer.

This focus on quality was nothing new for Haier. In 1985, in an incident that has since become part of Haier lore, one of the plant's customers came to Zhang Ruimin, then a plant manager, complaining about the shoddy quality of a refrigerator. To his dismay, when Zhang inspected the plant's inventory of four hundred refrigerators, he discovered that seventy-six refrigerators—one out of every five built by the plant—were just as defective. Zhang rounded up the faulty fridges, gathered the workforce, distributed sledgehammers, and ordered workers to smash them into bits. When they hesitated, he shouted, "Destroy them!" They did, and one of the sledgehammers is now on display at the company's headquarters.

But quality can be a moving target, as Haier has learned since its fridges and other appliances started competing in the United States with products from around the world. They have not always scored well on surveys conducted by *Consumer Reports*, an issue that Jemal has vowed to address. Yet, one of Haier's major contributions to the American market is as a new player in a field long dominated by familiar brand names—one that accurately anticipated the desire of the American consumer for new products, rather than just rely on what had worked in the American market for decades. In the long run, not only did Haier help diversify the American marketplace by introducing several new and innovative products; it also encouraged further innovation by fostering healthy competition, industry-wide.

It can't be denied that for American companies unwilling or unable to innovate and improve, competition from foreign players is sure to result in declining market share and profits. But isn't that the fundamental nature of a free-market economy? "Capitalism is fundamentally brutal, and competition will always breed winners and losers," Joe Nocera said. "Whenever a company like Tata or Haier tries to break into our market, they help to bring down prices and force American competitors to do things better and more efficiently." Nocera continued, "Yes, there are industries—like defense—where we need to have our own manufacturing base. But there aren't that many like that." Even within defense, competition is better for taxpayers than the monopoly that companies such as Boeing would prefer to enjoy.

Jemal, too, believes that competition from Haier has spurred its American competitors to improve—just as competition from Japanese auto companies forced Detroit to produce better, smaller, more fuel-efficient vehicles in the 1970s. In the future, Haier plans to ramp up its innovative efforts in the United States by improving its technical center so it can develop more appliances for American buyers and expanding its South Carolina campus, so it can build another assembly line for new products. "Net, net, net," Jemal concluded, "this is a plus for the U.S. economy."

Chapter Seven

THE
WELCOME MAT

I'm such a newcomer among all these people.

—CHRISTINA AGUILERA

On a Saturday night in October 2008, Georgetown, Kentucky, was hopping. Dozens of people strolled on its blocked-off downtown streets, listening to music, stopping at booths to buy cotton candy and caramel corn, settling in at tables and chairs for a chat with their neighbors. Just a few blocks away, almost every motel and hotel at the intersection of Interstate 75 and Cherry Blossom Way had a no-vacancy sign. Restaurants were bustling with patrons, and carloads of people lined up almost out to the street waiting for their turn in the Wendy's drive-through. The lively activity and commerce was a cheerful sign amid the gloom and anxiety of a financial downturn that had gripped the country.

It was striking to think that twenty years ago, almost none of this existed. In 1988, before Toyota opened the first of its plants here, Georgetown's small downtown consisted of empty store fronts and a few blocks of stately Victorian homes surrounding Georgetown College, the town's primary employer. Georgetown's main claim to fame, at least in Kentucky, was as "the birthplace of bourbon."

The only local hangout was a diner called Fava's, which boasted homemade pies, and the closest place to stay was in Lexington, fifteen miles away. The town could be reached by a single exit off I-75, which led visitors either into town or through rolling farmland. There was no place to eat, save for Fava's and a single McDonald's. There was certainly no evidence that Georgetown was about to become one of the premier centers of the automobile universe in the United States, let alone the world.

Today, Georgetown, a bustling suburb of twenty thousand, its streets lined with shops, restaurants, and parks, embodies everything that a community hopes will happen when a foreign manufacturer locates in their town. Indeed, companies from abroad are transforming and reinvigorating communities across the nation—from Columbus, Mississippi, to Mobile, Alabama, to Camden, South Carolina, to Chattanooga, Tennessee—in much the same way.

Despite whatever xenophobia might linger in some of these small cities and towns, it is impossible for their residents not to acknowledge how much they owe to the presence of a foreign company. And because economic reality generally trumps stubborn nationalist pride, people in these communities, particularly those that have struggled to keep homegrown employers from leaving, have begun to view foreign investment as a lifeline. They have come to realize that when a foreign-owned factory opens it doors, it does so much more than just create jobs; it stimulates local commerce, bolsters local businesses, and enriches the cultural foundation of the community and the communities surrounding it. On a smaller scale, a town can benefit in similar ways when a foreign company buys an existing American company and keeps its operations running, or when one opens a branch of its operations in the community. At a time when layoffs and plant closings happen every day at American companies, foreign companies are an alternative and, for some communities, the only option.

GEORGETOWN'S REVIVAL

In the past twenty years, Georgetown's population has doubled. At least a dozen new subdivisions have been built, including one neighborhood directly across the road from the Toyota complex, which employs 7,500 people and stretches for 2.7 miles along Cherry Blossom Way. Georgetown now also boasts a new recreation center, complete with an outdoor skateboard park, paid for by Toyota. The community has new elementary, middle, and high schools, and is expanding a Japanese garden. The Cincinnati Bengals hold summer practice in Toyota Stadium, also used by Georgetown College.

Downtown Georgetown now bustles with antique stores, an espresso bar (in the old bank building), and a new and improved Fava's, which recently got a face-lift and now sells T-shirts and postcards along with its meringue pies, which have been featured on the Food Network. The community is now home to three McDonald's restaurants and a *Walmart* Supercenter, and in just one cluster next to the interstate sit seven hotels—all built since the plant opened—along with restaurants such as Ruby Tuesday, Cracker Barrel, and Fazoli's, an Italian fast-food outlet.

Another thriving center of economic activity, equally as important, sits back from public view, in the Delaplain Industrial Park, just across Cherry Blossom from the Toyota complex. The complex includes a variety of business set up to support the Toyota plant, including Toyoda Machinery USA, which makes assembly line equipment; Aichi Forge USA, which makes the trucks that bring the materials and parts to the plant; and a branch of Louisville Forge and Gear Works, a steel manufacturer. But the biggest operation, set in a valley, is the Toyota Tsusho America complex, which produces everything from auto parts to chemicals and plastics. The industrial park also has logistics companies and a yard where the cabs for big eighteen-wheel trucks are stored. Across from all this sits a big white water tower, painted with the words "Georgetown: A Kentucky Treasure."

Georgetown's expansion is so legendary in economic development circles that other cities frequently send delegations to the town to study the impact that Toyota has had on the community; for example, officials from Tupelo, Mississippi, where Toyota is constructing a new assembly plant set to open in 2010, have already reached out to Georgetown for advice and guidance on what it can expect once its Toyota plant opens.

Yet, when the possibility of Toyota coming to Kentucky arose in the mid-1980s, some residents were less than thrilled. When former governor Martha Layne Collins made her first trip to Japan in the mid-1980s in an attempt to lure an automobile plant (following the example of her northern neighbor,

Ohio, whose former governor James Rhodes had convinced Honda to build two assembly plants and a technology center, and southern neighbor, Tennessee, which had attracted a Nissan plant), she faced a storm of criticism from residents and local lawmakers.

"Toyota is now accepted as part of the fabric of Kentucky, but it wasn't twenty years ago," said Dennis Cuneo, a longtime Toyota adviser. For one thing, the effort to attract Toyota was expensive for the financially challenged state. The $147 million incentive plan, which paid for acquiring land, preparing the site, and worker training, was thirty times what Ohio had paid to attract Honda (although half of what Alabama later spent to lure Mercedes-Benz), and Collins faced heat for spending so much money to attract a single employer. Beyond the costs, others were concerned that a Toyota plant would bring with it noise and unsightly construction, disrupting their sleepy little town.

So it was no surprise that despite Governor Collins's efforts to accommodate the company, Toyota officials themselves were greeted somewhat warily (at least at first) upon their arrival in Georgetown. One such executive was Fujio Cho, a manufacturing expert who was sent to become the plant's first president. But he didn't let this lukewarm reception faze him. He immediately began a charm campaign, attending weekly meetings of the Rotary Club, talking to residents about the company's plans, making sure that Toyota followed through on its initial promise to rebuild the Georgetown civic center. He and his wife, Emiko, whom he often accompanied on shopping trips to the local Kroger grocery store, soon became familiar figures, and Georgetown residents eventually accepted the Japanese couple among their own.

Cho, who later became Toyota's president and its chairman, learned the importance of community outreach early in his career. In the 1960s, a series of mudslides hit Tahara, Japan, a seaside town that was home to a Toyota assembly plant. Workers were unable to reach the factory, so it was forced to shut. Cho, who had been with the company for only four years, was working at the plant in Toyota's production control division. The company could not reach its employees—phone lines were down due to the disaster—so he traveled by boat throughout the neighborhoods where his workers lived, apologizing to them because the plant had closed and offering the company's help until they were back to work.

Twenty years and many promotions later, Cho was every bit as attentive to the concerns of his new community. He usually got an earful, in both his sessions with Kentucky officials and at the Rotary Club meetings. One frequent complaint concerned the growing amount of construction traffic that was entering and leaving the area, sometimes causing minor tie-ups on the roads around Georgetown.

"It was originally such a silent, peaceful town, and there was a great apprehension" about the one hundred to two hundred trucks per day that were visiting the site, Cho said. After asking town and county officials how they would remedy the situation, he simply asked construction companies serving the plant to avoid Frankfort Road, which goes through the heart of Georgetown, and to exit off I-75 onto roads leading straight to the plant site. "We instructed the truck drivers not to go through town— not to be an annoyance, and not to be a disruption," Cho said.

Toyota could not avoid irritating some community members who simply did not like the changes that were taking place.

At one Rotary Club meeting, an elderly member got up and launched into a lengthy rant about the foreign newcomers, getting "really, really angry," Cho said. He sat listening, feeling more than a little dismayed that there was such deep hostility toward Toyota after all of his efforts to reach out to—and become part of—the community. Cho went up the man afterward, expecting his tirade to continue. Instead, the man looked at him and said, "Oh, you are Japanese? I didn't even think of you as a Japanese man.'"

While Toyota is now a familiar and generally welcome presence, due in no small part to Cho's efforts, there are still some fears in the local community that its largesse could evaporate, given the slowdown in automobile sales that afflicted the industry late this decade. Residents of Georgetown cast a wary eye toward Princeton, Indiana, another Toyota town, where workers on one line in the assembly plant were off the job for months in 2008 and 2009, when the big pickups built there were sent to another factory. Indeed, temporary workers at the Georgetown plant were let go in 2009, and the company offered buyouts to encourage some older workers to leave and help reduce Toyota's costs. But given that Toyota has invested more than $5 billion in Georgetown, and brought about so many welcome changes, it has become pretty hard for residents to complain. "I'd do it again tomorrow," Collins said.

IN ANDERSON, CURING THE GM HANGOVER

By and large, the biggest impact of foreign investment on a community comes from a major projects, such as a car plant. Over the past twenty years, many such investments have gone to communities in the South, where local histories, customs, and cultures are not tied to a single industry or employer (like they are in Detroit), and a company can have a fresh start.

That would seem to count out Anderson, Indiana, a GM town for most of the past century. Against the odds, however, Anderson was able to win a factory from Nestlé, the Swiss food and confection giant. "I'm proud to be associated with this town and its people, who have excellent skills," said Paul Bulcke, the company's chief executive.

In Anderson's heyday, in the 1970s, one out of every three adult residents worked for GM in some capacity, making it second only to Flint, Michigan, where one out of two adults owed their jobs to the auto company. There were no fewer than twenty-four GM plants in Anderson, producing everything from lighting systems to electronic parts. Traffic was clogged day and night on Scatterfield Road, one of the city's main thoroughfares, so much so that the plants had to stagger their closing times so that workers didn't pour onto the roads all at once. Bar patrons at establishments such as the White Corner Bar stood three deep to get drinks after work, with a line of customers waiting outside.

In 1970, there were more than twenty-five thousand manufacturing jobs in Anderson, where the plants, like schools in New York City, were known by numbers, not by names. But during the 1990s, when GM's market share plummeted, one by one, the GM plants began to shut, and by the year 2000, those jobs had dropped by more than half to about eleven thousand. By 2006, the very last plant with a GM connection, a parts plant owned by its former components unit, the Delphi Corporation, shut its doors.

Perhaps no remaining structure is more symbolic of GM's tragic exit than the five-story, 1960s-era, pale-green-glassed administration building, now long empty. It sits on Scatterfield Road on a weed-choked lot, its entrance boarded up. But even though many of the GM plants are still up for sale, a foreign arrival has breathed new life into Anderson. If the Scatterfield Road building is a symbol of GM's demise, just outside of town now sits a building equally symbolic of its recovery: the Nestlé plant. In the starkest of contrasts with the deserted, sagging GM building, this state-of-the-art new plant bustles late into the evening as delivery trucks pull up to be loaded with cases of Nesquik milkshakes and Coffee-Mate nondairy creamer. Nestlé is here, in part, because of the efforts of Anderson's former mayor, Kevin Smith. During the middle of the decade, as he watched the former GM plants close, Smith decided he had to go outside the country in search of investment for his struggling town. He ordered business cards printed up in Chinese, Korean, and Japanese characters, and set off on a series of trade missions.

Smith was following an example set by the state's governor, Mitch Daniels, who was determined to change Indiana's image as a Rust Belt state. He made it clear that foreign investment was welcome in Indiana, no more so than when he privatized the east-west toll road that runs across the top of the state, between Ohio and Illinois, leasing the road to a concessions company formed as a joint venture between Cintra Concesiones de Infraestructuras de Transporte of Spain and Macquarie Infrastructure Group of Australia. Daniels scored other foreign investment, from Honda, which built a new small car plant in Greensburg, about an hour west of Cincinnati in the southwest part of the state, and from Toyota, which invested in Subaru's plant in Lafayette. Toyota stepped in after GM sold its share in Subaru's parent company, Fuji Heavy Industries. Together, those two auto companies added about three thousand new jobs to the state.

Nestlé's investment in Anderson wasn't nearly that significant. But for Anderson, where the population had dropped from seventy thousand in 1970 to less than fifty-eight thousand in the middle of this decade, the investment was a sign that Anderson residents could do more than just make car parts. In 2006, Nestlé agreed to build a $359 million, 880,000-square-foot plant, where it would employ three hundred people, on a former soybean field on the outskirts of town. In return, the city provided $46 million in tax breaks, and the state added another $7.8 million in incentives, mainly to be spent preparing the factory site and building roads around the plant.

While there was some grumbling about Nestlé's decision to use a fresh site—called a "greenfield location" in manufacturing terms—rather than locate in one of the old factories around town, that certainly didn't keep local residents from applying for jobs. When Nestlé executives set up shop in the historic Wigwam arena in downtown Anderson to conduct employment interviews, more than three thousand people showed up to apply. "There's a lot of enthusiasm and excitement in the area," Pam Krebs, a spokeswoman for Nestlé, said as the interviews were under way.

Nestlé told local officials that if the project worked out, it might expand the factory quickly. And it did so in 2008, announcing an expansion that would increase the size of the plant to 1.1 million square feet by 2011, and add another 135 jobs at the factory.

This might not seem like much compared to the thousands of jobs Toyota brought to Georgetown, but with an unemployment rate of 11.4 percent, several points above the national average, every new job was something for the people of Anderson to celebrate. To be sure, the positions at Nestlé do not pay as well as those at the former GM plants. Hourly wages range from $16.50 to $24 (with full benefits), whereas the last Delphi workers earned about $26 an hour, according to city officials. In addition, the Nestlé plant is nonunion, while most of the workers who had been employed by GM's plants were UAW members. (The workers at the Subaru/Toyota and Honda plants are nonunion, too; the union has never tried to organize either plant.)

So while the Nestlé plant alone is not enough to make up for the "GM hangover," as it was called in Anderson, what it provided for the town's residents, much more than jobs, was a glimmer of hope. "Anderson's on the move. And it's time," said longtime resident Dan Ferree, seventy-seven, one of the many people in Anderson who had worked for GM. Thanks to Nestlé, Ferree and his former GM coworkers were optimistic about Anderson's future, even if the employers were from outside the United States. "Everything changes," he said, with a shrug. "Change is good."

ENSURING A COMMUNITY'S FUTURE

Nearly five hundred miles south of Anderson, residents of Columbus, Mississippi, know firsthand that it can take a tremendous amount of hard work to lure and secure foreign investment for their community. But they've seen that the effort is well worth it. The story of Columbus's rebirth is a perfect example of how investment from abroad, however hard-won, can be the key to ensuring a better and brighter economic future for a community and those who call it home.

In literary circles, Columbus, a town of twenty-five thousand in the northeastern part of the state, equidistant from Memphis and Jackson, Mississippi, is best known as the hometown of playwright Tennessee Williams. It has streets lined with lovely 1920s homes and a quaint downtown that has been voted the prettiest in the South. When the rest of state was struggling to overcome the backwater image that stemmed from the civil rights era, Columbus seemed immune. "Our area has never been on top of the mountain, or on the bottom," said Bobby L. Harper, the retired president of Cadence Bank, a local institution.

For years, Columbus relied on two primary employers: its air force base, which trains one-third of military pilots in the United States, and a collection of manufacturing companies that dotted its landscape. But by the beginning of the twenty-first century, Columbus's economy was in danger of stalling. American manufacturers, who had moved to the South in search of lower costs and nonunion employees, were beginning to pull up stakes. More than five thousand jobs disappeared in two decades' time, including two thousand in 2003 alone, when the United Technologies factory in Columbus shifted its production of starter motors to Mexico. In 2005, when the Pentagon shuttered a number of military bases in the United States, the Columbus base was given a reprieve, but other facilities in Pascagoula and Vicksburg were not spared, and officials feared that Columbus would be next.

As economic problems grew, service at the area's small but

efficient airport began to shrink. Known as Golden Triangle Regional Airport, the compact facility might seem quaint to anyone used to battling crowds at LaGuardia or Los Angeles International; even with security restrictions that were added after the September 2001 attacks, it's possible to park, walk in the door, and board a plane in the space of ten minutes. Nevertheless, this diminutive airport turned out to be the key to Columbus's economic revival.

After 9/11, when the drop in air travel nationwide cost the airfield its daily flight to Dallas–Fort Worth, the Golden Triangle was left with only three daily flights on a Delta regional jet to Atlanta—miss a flight, and the only air travel alternative out of Columbus was to drive two hours to Jackson or Memphis. (At least Columbus still had service. In 2008, more than thirty communities across the United States were left without air service after cutbacks by struggling airlines.) Fearful that they could be left without daily flights, rendering the airport useless and stymieing local business (not to mention killing any chances of attracting new employers to the region), local leaders got creative. They began an effort to attract businesses to the airport property itself, which they hoped would create the traffic needed to keep Delta from leaving.

Much to their pleasant surprise, the property around the Golden Triangle Regional Airport proved to be quite attractive to foreign investors, who soon flocked to the region, transforming Columbus into one of the most popular and fastest-growing locations for foreign investment in the South. Since 2002, the land surrounding the airport has gone from an endless stretch of barren flatlands to a sea of construction sites housing hundreds of millions of dollars in new manufacturing plants.

Just across from the airport on Airport Road, the Russian steel company Severstal is building a mill that eventually will employ 2,800 people. Another new factory, built by Aurora Flight Sciences, an Israeli company, will produce unmanned aircraft and employ 300 people. PACCAR, the second biggest truck maker and parent company of Peterbilt, Kenworth, and DAF, the Dutch truck company, plans to open a diesel engine plant there in 2009. Meanwhile, the park's first two plants are already up and running: the American Eurocopter factories, owned by EADS.

In 2005, many residents of Mississippi became all too familiar with the bright orange rescue helicopters made at the Columbus plant; they were used by the coast guard to save Gulf residents trapped by rising floodwaters after Hurricane Katrina. But back in 2001, Nick Ardillo, then the airport's executive director, had no idea that EADS was looking for a site for helicopter production when he received a visit from Samuel Adcock, EADS's senior vice president for government affairs. Ardillo, who served as commander of the Columbus Air Force Base, already knew Adcock from his years in state government and assumed he was just paying a courtesy call to get reacquainted.

"I thought the visit was nice," Ardillo recalled in his musical Mississippi twang, "but I never thought anything would come of it." But he soon learned of the reason for Adcock's trip. In January 2002, after a nationwide search, EADS announced it would select a site in Mississippi for an American Eurocopter factory. The $11 million plant, which would employ one hundred workers, would assemble the AStar helicopter, used for everything from aerial photography and tours of Hawaiian volcanoes to radio and television station news reports. Ground breaking would take place in 2003, and EADS expected that the factory would be completed by 2004.

An automobile plant requires vast acreage and extensive construction, and can take years to complete, but the requirements for helicopter production are much simpler. Because parts are shipped in from elsewhere, and there are no components to manufacture, all the company would require was a site that could house a building several football fields long, no bigger than a giant warehouse, with an outdoor area for launch pads and testing stations.

There are no emissions from the factory because it uses none of the robotic welding or multiple processes that car plants employ; rather than travel along an automated assembly line, the helicopter bodies are mounted on movable workstations and progress down the factory floor on a palette that moves on wheels. "This is a clean business, and a very high-tech business," said Guy Hicks, the vice president for corporate communications at EADS North America. The fact that the operations are so contained, the process relatively uncomplicated, and the operations environmentally sound, made the investment even more attractive to Columbia officials.

INSIDE THE SALES PITCH

Marc Paganini, the chief executive of American Eurocopter, fell in love with the United States at age seventeen, when he traveled from France to become an exchange student at a high school in Philadelphia. Although he remains unmistakably French (despite his Italian last name), from his accent to his turn of phrase, Paganini is one of many executives born elsewhere who have honed their business skills working in America. His résumé includes a series of jobs as a finance expert and an investment banker, living in places such as Miami and New York. But his current job has taken him deep into the American South, to places such as Texas and Mississippi, and he divides his time between there and the company's headquarters in Grand Prairie, outside Dallas.

He joined EADS when part of the company was still owned by DaimlerChrysler. As EADS prepared to launch itself as an independent company, Paganini was given an enormous responsibility, that of preparing its listing on global stock exchanges. It was a job that required him to spend a lot of time in New York, where he felt very comfortable.

"We liked this country for a long time," he said of himself and his family. When the listing for EADS was completed, Paginini would have been a perfect choice to become the company's director of investor relations on Wall Street. But that did not interest him. "I told Philippe Camus," the CEO of EADS, "that I wanted to go back into operations," Paganini said.

And so he wound up in Texas. It might seem an adjustment for a Frenchman to land so far from the sophistication of Manhattan or the glitz of Miami, but Paganini said his family took almost immediately to the Lone Star State. For one thing, there is a sizable French community in Dallas, where Paganini has served as an officer of the area's French-American Chamber of Commerce, which holds Bastille Day celebrations, a Beaujolais festival, and regular symposiums from French-born businesspeople living in the region. "We are really enjoying living in Texas," he said.

There is also a significant aerospace community in the area, which is home to two big airlines—American and Southwest—and one of EADS's biggest competitors, Bell Helicopter. As he began to work with employees at the American Eurocopter operations in Grand Prairie, Paganini noticed that many had a considerable understanding of the aerospace business, something that proved to be an advantage as the company looked for workers to recruit.

But the location was something of a drawback, too. Paganini and other EADS executives learned that Bell Helicopter already had a grip on the hearts and minds of people in the state, as well as its congressional delegation. Although Texas politicians gave the EADS officials their time and consideration, it was clear that their loyalties, at best, would be divided. When American Eurocopter went looking to build its new factory in the South, Paganini wanted to choose a location where the company would be considered a favorite son, not part of an extended family. He zeroed in on Mississippi.

Once Mississippi communities learned EADS had chosen their state as the home for its new plant, "The food fight was on," Ardillo said. In Columbus, the members of the airport's board said, "Let's go after it, and we went after it like there was no tomorrow," he said. The state would provide some assistance, but it then was up to individual development agencies and towns to sell themselves to EADS. Officials began to arrive from France and Germany for tours and meetings, during which Columbus officials missed no opportunity to tout the advantages of their site.

For one thing, they told their prospective investors, it was located at an airport, meaning that EADS could test the helicopters at a site used to aviation activity. Plus, there were numerous academic facilities in the region, including Mississippi State University in Starkville (home to the Bagley College of Engineering, used by General Electric as an incubator for jet engine development), just a few miles away.

The local officials also touted the cultural and recreational facilities in the area, including Columbus's quaint downtown and the elegant Old Waverly Golf Club in nearby West Point, whose course can be played virtually year-round, thanks to the region's temperate weather. The Columbus team also stressed the availability of affordable, attractive homes in both Starkville (where Johnny Cash had famously spent a night in jail), and Columbus. In both places, a modern four-bedroom home on an acre of land can cost less than $200,000, and taxes are a little more than $1,000 a year.

On their third visit, EADS officials seemed impressed, Harper said. But, as the group was heading to Old Waverly for a round of golf, they surprised their local hosts by cutting to the chase. "Let's talk money. What can you do?" Harper recalls being asked. The Golden Triangle group hadn't realized that the EADS visitors were expecting an answer that day. They were looking for a local investment of $7 million, which would pay for a site that ideally could hold a 100,000-square-foot building—even though the initial structure might turn out to be much smaller. The company wanted the local officials to construct the building and would then lease it back over twelve years.

But there were two problems for the Golden Triangle group: the site the airport authority had in mind could hold a facility with no more than 87,500 square feet, and moreover, the money was not yet there. Harper instructed Ardillo to keep the group out on the road as long as possible, then went to work, securing the $7 million in financing pledges over the phone and writing up a hasty proposal whose last copies were still being stapled just as the EADS group pulled up at the country club. (They kept their fingers crossed that their slightly small site would be acceptable.)

The effort kept Columbus in the running, and the board members went to work, raising the money from eleven different sources. Local and county governments pledged grants, and the state promised to provide assistance to the winning bidder. Yet Ardillo was uneasy about the rush to put together a proposal. "I realized, we're doing a great job of coming in second place," he said.

He needn't have worried. Beyond the financial package, EADS officials told the group they were impressed by the area's educational resources, especially the aerospace engineering laboratory that has been in operation at Mississippi State since 1934. Proximity to higher education has been a strong selling point to many foreign companies, who often look to the local scholars for technical and financial expertise, in deciding where to put American facilities. Honda chose Marysville, Ohio, in part because of its proximity to the Ohio State University; Toyota chose Georgetown because of its local college and the University of Kentucky in nearby Lexington, while Mercedes was drawn to Vance, Alabama, because it was just down the road from the University of Alabama.

Even though the site was a little smaller than they had hoped for, officials at EADS were also swayed by an offer by East Mississippi Community College to create training programs specifically for American Eurocopter workers. The visitors from Germany and France also liked the surrounding community, dotted with well-maintained homes from the 1920s and 1930s, and they particularly enjoyed the Old Waverly Golf Club. During one dinner, a deer sauntered across the golf course, pausing as if on cue to gaze in at the EADS group.

But perhaps what really clinched the deal was that the Europeans simply appreciated the effort that the Columbus group had made. "What struck me at that time was the willingness of the people to have us there. They were working hard to help us to come," said Paganini. And with good reason. In 2004, after EADS announced that Golden Triangle had won the project, the first in what would be a series of new developments at the airport, "You could see the bounce in peoples' steps," Ardillo said. "After we realized we can compete for a world-class company, we could compete for anything." And they have, landing a second American Eurocopter factory, the steel mill, diesel engine factory, and drone plant.

EADS proved useful for the Golden Triangle leaders, who used the plant as a linchpin in their fund-raising efforts to attract even more investment. They devised an economic development plan that included a marketing campaign, a government affairs representative, and the purchase of computer tools to showcase the remaining plant sites. The goal of the outreach campaign was to raise at least $1.5 million from area communities. Instead, they wound up with $2.2 million in donations. "It was the easiest fund raising ever," said Harper.

Despite all that EADS has done for the community, Ardillo acknowledged some local residents still feel uneasy at seeing foreign influences surface in Columbus. But to those who question why foreign investment was necessary, he has a quick answer:

"Read *The World Is Flat*," he says. In time, residents have come to realize that Columbus's future lies with investors from abroad. For the most part, "Mississippians have embraced the idea that it is a global economy, and that there is not a problem with having international companies invest in the state," said Gray Swoope, the state's director of economic development. "They're spending money. They're investing in the community. They're in our schools; they're in our churches. They're bringing a whole new vitality," added Bobby Harper.

As the helicopter plants hum and construction continues, the impact is only beginning to be felt. But there's no question that EADS's investment has bestowed upon the city of Columbus a new vitality, saving it from falling into economic obscurity and offering it the promise of a bright and prosperous future. And as we will see in the next chapter, while no community's future can be forever assured, the promise of becoming another Georgetown, or winning investments like those at the Golden Triangle, is enough to keep state lawmakers on the prowl.

Chapter Eight

THE RACE
BETWEEN
THE STATES

A community needs a soul if it is to become a true home for human beings. You, the people, must get it this soul.

—POPE JOHN PAUL II

While the efforts of local and community officials can go a long way in attracting foreign investment to a region, no one yields more power in that situation than a state's governor. He or she is the rainmaker, the game clincher, and the face of the state that is striving to attract a company from Japan, China, Germany, India, or elsewhere. While a state's legislature might also have a say, the governor provides the leadership and can often direct economic development funds or even money designated for use by the executive office to sweeten a deal. And they do, because no matter their party, most governors in the United States believe that foreign investment benefits their states, their communities, and their constituents (no surprise, given that foreign companies are present in every state in the union).

Thus, many go after it with ambassadorial zeal. Some critics say that in doing so, they are selling their state to overseas investors, but in reality they are buyers more than they are sellers.

In securing foreign investment, they are buying a better economic future for their states and their constituents.

STRANGE BEDFELLOWS

Of all the American governors who have been aggressive in fighting for foreign investment during this past decade, two stand out: Jennifer Mulhern Granholm, a Democrat from Michigan, and Haley Reeves Barbour, the Republican governor of Mississippi. Granholm, who represents a northern industrial state, and Barbour, from a rural southern one, could not seem more different in political outlook and economic priorities (let alone personal background), but when it comes to foreign investment, their goals are essentially the same.

Granholm, who helped train Vice President Joe Biden in the 2008 debate preparation sessions, has close ties to President Barack Obama and served on his transition team. Barbour, on the other hand, is the former chairman of the Republican National Committee, led the GOP's efforts to recapture the House and Senate during the 1990s, and had close ties to both former presidents Bush. Except for national governors' conferences, it is unlikely that these two have spent very much time in each other's company, nor do they agree on many policy issues or agendas.

Yet their shared determination to bring jobs and capital to their states has linked them in a common purpose. Each has been willing to take bold steps that few politicians from their states might have risked in the past. Each has gone right to the doorstep of corporations outside the United States, personally knocking on doors in Tokyo, Seoul, and Frankfurt and using their considerable public aplomb to make passionate appeals to foreign companies to build factories and research centers in their states. While their efforts have been met with varying levels of success, both have results to show for it: Granholm and Barbour each can claim a major investment from Toyota, Barbour has attracted EADS's American Eurocopter plant, and both states have won engineering investments from a variety of foreign firms. For Granholm, whose state has lost 750,000 jobs since 2000 due to the auto industry's decline, the situation is desperate and the need for investment is dire. As she said in a hoarse voice when she opened a new Toyota research center in 2008: "Michigan is open for business. Michigan welcomes international business." In Mississippi, battered by Hurricane Katrina and with one of the lowest rates of college graduation and literacy in the country, the future also hangs in the balance. But because Mississippi lacks the vocal and powerful opponents of foreign investment that Michigan has in the UAW and the auto industry, Barbour has been politically bolder than Granholm can ever afford to be.

BARBOUR'S PERSONAL APPEAL

Late in 2006, Haley Barbour sat in front of a video camera to make a final impassioned pitch to land the new assembly plant that Toyota planned to build in North America. Mississippi had fought long and hard against the other two finalists, Tennessee and Arkansas, for the $1.3 billion project, and with good reason. The state that emerged victorious would not only win the plant itself, which would provide two thousand new jobs, but also the foreign parts suppliers that undoubtedly would build factories near the facility, providing thousands more jobs. Now, in his honeyed southern accent, Barbour presented the state's selling points to an elite audience of Toyota executives who would watch the video in Japan and make the final decision.

"Welcome to the center of the new automotive universe," Barbour said. "I want to remind you why the state of Mississippi is the right economic and political partner for Toyota." Dressed in a dark suit, a bright green tie, and proudly displaying a pin with the American and Japanese flags in his lapel, Barbour narrated a four-minute video that seemed as much a travel brochure as it was an economic proposal.

There were photographs of lush, rolling hills and farms, and footage of the state's most notable celebrities: Eudora Welty, the Pulitzer Prize–winning author from Jackson, and, of course, Elvis Presley, who was born in Tupelo. The shots of Mississippi residents depicted a carefree, diverse community, where children toddled beside their parents at farmer's markets spilling over with bushels of green beans and sweet corn. (This was meant to catch the eye of Japanese executives, whose overcrowded and less fertile country rarely allowed for such agricultural abundance.)

Standing in front of the state seal, Barbour glossed over the state's perennially dismal record on education and touted Mississippi's lower taxes, superior geography, and proximity to other new plants built by Mercedes-Benz, Honda, Hyundai, Nissan, and Kia. And, in a tip to Toyota's emphasis on the environment, Barbour promised to declare Toyota Arbor Day on the date the plant was dedicated, promising that every schoolchild in Mississippi would plant a tree in the company's honor that day. He gazed into the camera with the same determined look that had become familiar to Americans who had seen him on Sunday morning talk shows back when he led the RNC in the mid-1990s.

In a voice redolent with southern charm, Barbour wound up his pitch. "Mississippi will use its political skills and strength to be a good partner and strong ally to Toyota." He pledged the support in Washington of the state's congressional delegation, led by Senator Trent Lott, the former Republican leader.

"When some in Washington try to change the rules harmful in ways to Toyota and the new domestics, we will fight for you—during and after the Bush Administration," Barbour said. "We're committed to Toyota/Tupelo becoming your company's most productive plant in North America. It's not only in your best interest, but our best interest. Thank you for your time," the governor concluded. "We can't wait to begin."

Barbour's video seemed the crowning moment in a massive effort that had by then taken years and involved many players— not only Barbour, but Mississippi's state legislature, the four counties near the plant site, and the Tupelo business community. The multiyear effort to land Toyota began even before official word emerged that the company was looking for a site for its eighth North American assembly plant. Shortly after he was elected in 2004, Barbour, who had seen the economic growth that EADS and other foreign investors had brought to the Golden Triangle region, contacted Dennis Cuneo, then Toyota's senior vice president, who was in charge of finding a site for the plant. "From the very first, we targeted Toyota," Barbour told me. Mississippi had failed to impress Toyota two years earlier, when Tupelo had lost out to San Antonio as the location for a pickup truck plant; determined not to be stung again, Barbour was now ready to pull out all the stops.

In August 2005, a year and a half after taking office, Barbour and a delegation from the state traveled to Nagoya, Japan, to visit the international exposition hosted by Aichi Prefecture, Toyota's home state. Barbour then traveled the hour-long trip to Toyota City to pay his own courtesy call on Katsuaki Watanabe, who had just become Toyota's chief executive. There was no project to promote, simply hands to shake, but the seeds had been planted.

KATRINA STRIKES

Two weeks after Barbour's trip to Japan, Hurricane Katrina tore through the state, devastating Mississippi towns such as Bay St. Louis, Biloxi, and Gulfport. Bridges collapsed, houses were leveled, and businesses were destroyed. Even after stranded residents had been rescued, the carnage cleared, and rebuilding efforts were under way, the long journey to repair the economy of Mississippi's Gulf Coast had just begun.

With their state's infrastructure devastated and its regional economy wiped out, Mississippi officials knew the state was an unlikely candidate for the foreign investment it would need to get back on its feet. Among other concerns, state officials worried that the investors that they had been courting would view Mississippi through the same lens as its beleaguered neighbor, Louisiana, which seemed unable to lift itself, literally and figuratively, out of the debris from the storm. "How are we going to respond? A lot of these companies are going to think that we've been wiped off the map," Swoope worried.

Barbour had an answer. On the Friday after Katrina battered the state, Barbour asked Swoope for a list of companies to call. This list included Toyota. The next Sunday evening, he phoned Swoope at home with a status report. Swoope said to the governor, "It's eight-thirty at night, who is there to talk to?" Barbour replied, "It's ten-thirty Monday morning in Asia." Barbour, it turned out, had spoken to officials at Nissan, Toyota, and others he had courted and convinced them that Mississippi's cleanup efforts were well under way. Despite what they might see on international newscasts, he urged them to remember that Mississippi still wanted their investments and that the state could still give them any information they needed. Those efforts, Swoope said, "created some kind of bond with companies like Toyota. If there was a silver lining to Katrina, it was that it exposed the true spirit of Mississippi. We are a resilient people who can bounce back."

In May 2006, a month after the *New York Times* ran a story disclosing that Toyota was planning to build a new factory in one of four southern states (Virginia, Tennessee, Arkansas, or North Carolina), Barbour traveled to New York and invited Cuneo to come and look at locations in Mississippi. One was the site outside Tupelo, now called Wellspring, that Toyota had seen before and declared to be not construction ready. But Barbour wasn't about to let history repeat itself; he had had Tupelo officials carve out detritus from the land where the plant would sit, and had the property precertified by the Tennessee Valley Authority as a "megasite," appropriate for a major development.

Cuneo arrived there in July 2006, and after touring the site and listening to a sales pitch from the governor and local development and community leaders, he came away with new regard for the region. The Toyota official was particularly impressed by one statistic: 32.4 percent of unemployed people within sixty miles of the plant had worked in manufacturing (compared with 17 percent in Georgetown, 11.8 percent in Buffalo, West Virginia, and only 7.6 percent in San Antonio, the home to Toyota's newest plant), which meant Toyota would be able to attract a workforce already acclimated to working in factories, saving the time and expense of teaching workers step by step as it was doing in Texas and elsewhere. Also, the site was only ninety minutes from the Memphis International Airport, a hub for Northwest Airlines, and close to a series of cross docks in Memphis that Toyota used to sort parts for just-in-time delivery to its plants in Kentucky and elsewhere. The area lacked an interstate highway, but Mississippi officials promised they would lobby hard for U.S. 78 to be turned into one, if the project came about.

But Mississippi was still not even on Toyota's official consideration list—and the press was speculating that Toyota would pick Arkansas or Tennessee, whose governors were already claiming victory. So Barbour ramped up his efforts, traveling again to Tokyo to speak at a conference on disaster relief, where he touted his state's recovery efforts in the wake of Katrina. Visiting Toyota executives relayed their impressions of Barbour's report back to Toyota's CEO, and in fall 2006, Cuneo added the Wellspring site to his list of sites.

A key factor in putting Mississippi into contention was the incentive package Barbour had assembled. Victory was not cheap, costing the state $294 million in incentives, or $147,000 for each of the two thousand jobs the plant would create (similar to what Arkansas and Tennessee were offering but much less than Alabama had previously paid for factories from Mercedes-Benz and Hyundai). Of that, $146.9 million paid for infrastructure, such as rail lines to the plant site, frontage roads, roads inside the plant grounds, a highway exit, water and sewer service, and communication lines for telephone and Internet. Another $67 million went for the site preparation, and $80 million was set aside for workforce training. The state also said it would cover Toyota's marketing expenses when the plant opened. To Barbour and other state officials, it was worth every penny. "Certainly Toyota benefits from it," said Swoope, the state's economic development director, "but so do the people of Mississippi."

At the ground breaking two months later, Watanabe and Barbour, both former amateur baseball players, picked up shovels to toss aside the first loads of bright brick-red soil. Barbour hosted a welcoming dinner that included grilled Kobe-style beef from cattle raised in Texas and a centerpiece featuring branches of cherry blossoms, the beloved Japanese flower—a meal appropriately symbolic of the happy marriage of the two cultures.

Still, some predicted that Mississippi residents would be uncomfortable with Toyota's presence. For example, Marty Russell, a weekly columnist for the *Northeast Mississippi Daily Journal*, wrote, "I don't know much about the Japanese or their culture. I know they eat raw fish, produce weird, big-eyed cartoon characters and live on a crowded island that is prone to earthquakes and being stomped flat by mutant lizards with radioactive halitosis." In general, however, the Tupelo community was welcoming. "We're a very warm, hospitable state," Barbour said. "People are excited to see them. This is a very big deal."

To make their Japanese visitors feel even more at home, the University of Mississippi in Oxford, about thirty miles away, started a Saturday school at Toyota's request so that the children of company officials could study their native language and other home customs. And when high oil prices and shifts in Toyota's strategy indefinitely delayed the plant's scheduled opening in 2008, Barbour remained committed to his new partners, making yet another trip to Japan to assure Toyota officials his state would do whatever it took to make the factory successful.

After all, "We've got just as big a stake in this plant being successful as they do," said Barbour. As with any high-stakes gamble, he will have to wait a while to see if his bet pays off.

MICHIGAN'S SEARCH FOR JOBS

In Michigan, however, Granholm's considerable efforts have proved somewhat less successful, as she has run into considerable resistance from the UAW (a key supporter in her election for two terms), and from her own constituents. As one might expect in a state so long dominated by GM, Ford, and Chrysler, in Michigan, the reaction to foreign investment—particularly by auto companies—has been somewhat less than hospitable. There are still signs at the headquarters of the United Auto Workers union rudely instructing owners of foreign cars to park elsewhere. And no one has forgotten that in the 1980s, local charities put on fund raisers in which the frustrated could take a sledgehammer to the hood of a foreign car—three swings for a dollar. In a much more sobering incident in 1982, a Chinese-

American waiter named Vincent Chin was murdered by a Chrysler worker and his stepson—who mistook him for Japanese.

Despite having all these odds against her, Granholm vowed, soon after taking office in 2003, that she would "go anywhere and do anything" to bring jobs to Michigan. After all, she needed to land every job she could, as, during her tenure, the American automotive industry went into a tailspin. When Granholm took office in 2003, her state's biggest employers, GM, Ford and Chrysler, were in freefall, thanks in part to decades of mismanagement and an inability to keep up with the changing tastes of the American consumer, which I wrote about in my previous book, *The End of Detroit: How the Big Three Lost Their Grip on the American Car Market.*

From 2003 to 2008, Michigan carmakers alone cut more than 280,000 jobs, shuttering plants and factories across the state, and leading to hundreds of thousands more job losses. During Granholm's time in office, unemployment in Michigan ranked as the worst in the nation, soaring above 10 percent. The state ranked as high as fifth in home foreclosures, and it was dead last in the country in attracting new residents. For Granholm, who was forced to implement an unpopular tax increase, the only salvation to be found was from overseas.

In her first five years in office, Granholm went on seven grueling foreign trade missions, including three to Japan, in pursuit of foreign investors. On one three-day trip to Japan in September 2008, Granholm visited five cities—Tokyo, Yokohama, Nagoya, Aichi, and Osaka—and met with executives at twenty-three companies. Some were big auto companies such as Toyota, Honda, and Mazda, but Granholm also paid visits to Sharp Electronics; the photo-imaging giant Konica Minolta;

Howa, the textile manufacturer; and Terumo, which produces medical equipment. Some already had operations in the state, while others were on her wish list. "We've got to transform Michigan," she said. "Change is imperative."

But unfortunately for Granholm, and for the residents of Michigan, the change she fought so hard to bring to her state could not completely offset the devastation that the auto industry had wrought. Though her missions managed to attract thirty-seven companies and $800 million in investments, this amounted to only nine thousand jobs—or about 3 percent of the jobs lost in the state during that same period. Moreover, GM and Chrysler filed for bankruptcy in 2009, which she had warned would be a disaster for the state. To be fair, few experts felt Michigan would ever return to the stature it once held in the twentieth century as a wealthy boom state, where residents earned thousands of dollars more than the national average.

The formidable challenges Granholm faces in her quest to bring foreign investment to her state can be best demonstrated by her failed 2006 bid for a Toyota engine plant. At the time, Toyota was looking for a place to manufacture the engines for the Highlander crossover SUVs it originally planned to build in Mississippi. Convincing the company to build this factory in Michigan was a long shot, but Granholm gave it the same indefatigable effort that had won her state a $150 million Toyota safety center earlier that year. As soon as she'd caught wind that real estate developers planned to purchase a site she had in mind for the center, she immediately went to court to win an injunction barring the sale. She then convinced local lawmakers to approve the incentive package that ultimately secured the land.

On one trade mission to Japan, she visited Nagoya, where

she presented Toyota with her list of potential sites and stressed the state's advantages, emphasizing an ample supply of skilled workers who already knew the industry and would not need the kind of training that employees at other Toyota factories had needed. Toyota officials feared, and rightly so, that the Detroit companies would be far from pleased to see the Japanese automaker in their state, so Granholm did all she could to assuage their concerns. "We want to make sure they know how welcome they would be," Granholm told me.

As a courtesy to the governor, Cuneo looked at several of the sites, most seriously at the one off I-69 south of I-94, just north of the Michigan-Indiana border. The site met many of the company's criteria. But there was one major drawback: the strong presence in the state of the United Auto Workers union. The UAW's president, Ron Gettelfinger, said he would not try to block the Toyota plant (adding that it would benefit the state), but a number of Toyota officials in the United States had no doubt that if the plant was built in Michigan, the UAW would immediately launch a campaign to sign up its workers, just as it had tried to do over the years in Georgetown, Kentucky.

Cuneo, meanwhile, had even more doubts. He thought it highly unlikely that the state's politicians, many of whom didn't have a shot at reelection without support from the union, would ever embrace Toyota as enthusiastically as they did their homegrown automobile companies. Quite simply, in a state that so revolved—politically and economically—around the American auto companies, Toyota just couldn't expect the same support it had elsewhere. "We had [Mississippi Senator] Trent Lott saying he is going to be a warrior for Toyota," Cuneo remarked. "I don't think a Michigan senator would ever say that." (In fact, his view was born out in 2008, when Michigan's lawmakers lost their battle for congressional assistance. One of the state's senators, Debbie Stabenow, grew so openly upset over the backlash against her state's once-mighty coalition of carmakers that she had to be comforted by her colleagues.)

Still, the state's bid was given serious consideration by Toyota's American managers, who were charged with making a recommendation back to Japan. Several executives involved in the decision were in favor of putting the engine plant in Michigan; others strongly opposed it. In the end, that lack of consensus caused Granholm to lose her case. If even the Americans at Toyota could not present a unanimous recommendation to Japan for approval, company officials reasoned, there was no possibility that the already nervous Japanese officials could be convinced of the wisdom of putting the factory in such a controversial place.

Granholm, who saw her approval rating drop below 40 percent in 2009, admitted that her efforts at courting foreign investors had been difficult for her constituents to accept—and that intellectual considerations were overwhelmed by gut reactions. "The pace of global change has been at the speed of light. People haven't quite caught up with that. There is an emotional, and rightly so, feeling to being patriotic," Granholm said, acknowledging that Michigan residents had every right to hold up their past as proof of the state's contribution to the American economy. "We're a tough people, a scrappy people, but change is hard. People are losing homes and jobs and they're tough on us," she added. "If anybody can realize the world has changed, it's Michigan. We are the poster child for having been impacted by globalization."

Still, in foreign investment, she sees a way for her state to remain a player, and she hasn't given up yet. In November 2008, on the eve of a vote in Congress on the auto industry bailout, Granholm was off on another trade mission in a completely different direction, to Israel and Kuwait, countries that, without an auto industry presence, don't evoke the same stigma or protectionist rhetoric in Detroit as Japan. She hoped Michigan's large population of Arab-Americans and its sizable Jewish community would give her strong selling points in luring investors from the Middle East. Still challenges remain, for, to many investors from the Middle East and elsewhere, Michigan is and always will be an auto state. "We're doing everything possible, not just to reshape the economy but to reshape people's expectations about what Michigan is," she said.

Yet Granholm has seen firsthand how difficult it is to walk both sides of the line. When her home-state industry was on its knees, she ultimately was forced to choose sides. During the congressional bailout debate, she became a passionate defender of GM, Ford, and Chrysler, declaring that the failure to approve support was "unAmerican." She continued to speak out for them when GM and Chrysler veered close to bankruptcy the following spring. But perhaps the most public proof of her support came in January 2009, when she took part in a mini-parade on the floor of the Detroit Auto Show. Clad in a vivid red pantsuit and cheered on by GM retirees and employees, she carried a sign that read, "We're Electric" on one side and "Here to Stay" on the other. For anyone who knew about Granholm's efforts to court foreign businesses, the scene would seem to indicate that she was trying to have it all.

Granholm's balancing act—trying to protect Detroit carmakers while still going after the foreign money she needs to keep her state afloat—highlights a fundamental challenge that faces political leaders across the country, especially those in states dominated by big unions. Governors everywhere remain duty bound to promote their homegrown firms (if not out of loyalty than out of political expediency), especially in their deepest time of need. But in today's global marketplace, they simply cannot guarantee economic survival and prosperity for their states without attracting investment from overseas. For Granholm, Barbour, and other governors across the nation, the real goal isn't to sell their states to foreign investors, it's to sell their constituents on the importance—in truth, the necessity—of letting global players into their fray.

Chapter Nine

A VIEW
FROM THE TOP

All that we are arises with our thoughts. With our thoughts, we make the world.

—PRINCE SIDDHARTHA GAUTAMA (BUDDHA)

W hether a company is based in California or Calcutta, doing business in the United States isn't easy. The American market is one of the biggest, most complicated, and most challenging in the world. For a foreign-owned company, faced with the additional challenge of winning over American hearts and minds, the obstacles are even more difficult to surmount. In order to be accepted as a true player in the American economy, it isn't always enough to just hire American workers, invest money in American communities, and introduce news skills, products, and technologies to the American marketplace. To succeed in the United States, foreign-owned companies must strive to integrate themselves not only into our economy, but into the very fabric of our culture and society as well—to be seen, in essence, as the equivalent of an American company.

Toyota has taken on that task with a zeal and singularity of purpose that no other foreign company has ever attempted.

While its executives never deny that it is, first and foremost, a Japanese company, they have gone out of their way to weave Toyota into the fabric of America. We have already looked at the steps that Toyota has taken with individual workers and managers, in local communities, and in Washington. But in order to really understand how Toyota has approached the American market, it was necessary for me to go to Japan and talk to the men (for there are no women with any sizable influence at the company) who have set the policies that Toyota has followed in its effort to be embraced by the American public.

Toyota, among all the foreign companies that do business in the United States, stands alone in recognizing that buying into the American economy was the key to turning it into one of the world's most important global companies. Because of its incredible success here, its actions have been studied by all manner of companies, from Haier and Tata to JetBlue and Southwest Airlines. On one hand, it frustrates and perplexes some American executives, who wonder how a company with such simple principles and such a transparent global strategy could have played the game better than they do. But on the other, they can't help but admit that in Toyota there is much to emulate. Here is a look at the men who have been instrumental in laying out the steps that Toyota has taken and the part it has played in remaking the American dream.

THE NEW WORLD OF TOYOTA

Nagoya, Japan, sits about 160 miles west of Tokyo, a two-and-a-half-hour ride on the bullet train, or *shinkansen*. With more than two million people, Nagoya is the country's third largest city. In 1610, roughly a decade before the pilgrims arrived at Plymouth Rock, Tokugawa Ieyasu, one of Japan's most powerful shoguns, selected what became Nagoya as the site for his castle, an imposing structure that remains the city's main tourist attraction, particularly in cherry blossom season. By and large, however, the reason most people travel here is to visit Toyota, which has turned Nagoya and the surrounding region into the base for its global automotive empire.

Until recently, visitors to Nagoya would not have had an inkling that such a powerful global company was based here. Consistent with Japanese values of understatement and modesty, Toyota's corporate operations were originally divided between a nondescript mid-rise office building in the center of the city, a skyscraper in Tokyo near the Tokyo Dome indoor sports arena, and a small low-rise building at its manufacturing complex in Toyota City, thirty-five miles from Nagoya. While the Tokyo skyscraper was impressive, the other buildings seemed dingy, out of date, and certainly not the best face to present to the world. As Toyota's operations have grown more global—that is to say, more American—all that has changed.

Toyota's gleaming new thirty-nine-story global headquarters building sits just across the street from the train station, on one of the busiest corners in Nagoya, visible for miles in the surrounding area. The first time I stepped inside, I was expecting an anonymous lobby and perhaps a modest sign saying "Toyota." Not so. Luxury shops such as Cartier, Loewe, and Fortnum and Mason fill the first floor, while gourmet restaurants such as Enotecca Pinchiorri, an outpost of the famed establishment from Florence, Italy, can be found on floors higher up. To the naked eye, it could just as easily be a skyscraper in Los

Angeles, New York, or Chicago—or perhaps one in Singapore or Bangkok, where so much new construction has taken place over the past decade. To my surprise, there was nothing to indicate that Toyota is one of the tenants—no big gleaming gold letters inside, or out, that shout its presence. If you want to get to the inner hub of this global empire, you have to know where to look, and that means a walk along the far western wall to a private bank of elevators whose cars travel directly, and silently, to the twenty-fourth floor. It is here that visitors step out and into the new world of Toyota.

Uniformed receptionists immediately greet newcomers, who must show identification and receive a badge that will eventually allow them upstairs, to the floors where Toyota's offices are housed. Beyond the reception desk is a lavish two-story lobby, trimmed in walnut paneling and brushed aluminum fittings, with a sweeping, panoramic view of downtown Nagoya—exactly the kind of atmosphere that a powerful global company could be expected to present. There are tables and chairs and sofas, and a scene that looks something like a waiting room at the United Nations.

Well-dressed Japanese visitors mingle with Westerners, switching languages at ease—from Japanese and English to Portuguese, Arabic, and Russian. In one glance, it is clear that the understatement that long marked the company's offices is no longer appropriate for the world's biggest carmaker—and one of the world's richest companies.

But far more than a reminder of the company's success, the revamped Toyota headquarters are a symbol of how its identity has been shaped by its new global position. Just as American workers, communities, governors, and statesmen have been affected by Toyota's presence, so, too, has the culture of Toyota been influenced by its American experience. To truly comprehend the impact of the company on our own economy and society it is critical to gain an understanding of just how the two cultures—ours and Toyota's—have become so intertwined.

TOYOTA'S AMERICAN PITCHMAN

Precisely on the dot of our appointed interview time, a door opened, and in strode Fujio Cho, the chairman of Toyota, still hearty at seventy-two. He broke into a smile and greeted me in the English he perfected while running Toyota's plant in Georgetown, Kentucky, although he spoke in Japanese during the meeting and relied on a translator to make his points. In Cho, Toyota had its first chairman ever to have run an operation in the United States and the first to have grappled with the challenges that face foreign companies when they enter communities across America. Cho became the first Japanese executive who many American journalists—and indeed American politicians, community leaders, and at least half the company's employees—ever got to know on a regular basis (our Nagoya meeting was one of at least half a dozen such interviews over the past twenty years). It is Cho, truly an embodiment of the company's living history, who can be credited with taking the first steps to carve out a place for Toyota in Americans' hearts and minds, though he has faced his fair share of challenge along the way.

Just as Granholm and Barbour have been ambassadors to Toyota for their states, Cho has been something of an ambassador to the United States for Toyota. Ever since well before the company built its first cars here, he has been both pitchman for the company and advocate for the United States, selling not only Toyota on the idea of America, but America on the idea of Toyota. At a time when Japanese executives rarely appeared on American stages or mingled with the American public, Cho took on the job with determination, even when Japanese companies were being rattled by protectionist sentiment and warned they would face a hostile response if they came here.

One of Cho's first visits was in 1980, when, as a middle-ranking manager, he traveled to Detroit to speak to a group of industry engineers about the methods and principles of the Toyota Production System. This is the heart and soul of the way that Toyota operates, and Cho was one of the best people on the planet to explain it. He had worked directly with the system's inventor, Taiichi Ohno, and had been practicing the system for almost twenty years. But executives in Japan thought long and hard about allowing Cho to go, said James P. Womack, a manufacturing expert who has studied Toyota for decades. Until then, the production system had been something of a secret—not because Toyota wanted to keep its methods under wraps but because it wasn't sure that it could explain it with any meaning for outsiders.

Cho got the go-ahead to travel to Detroit, and he gave a speech that outlined the way Toyota worked. Looking back now, it seems pretty amazing that the meeting, which attracted about five hundred people, drew almost no public attention at the time. Not realizing that Cho had just lifted the curtain on a company that scores of executives, academics, and journalists—such as myself—would spend years trying to dissect, members of the group, now known as the Association for Manufacturing

Excellence, simply left the meeting confused. They had no idea what Cho meant when he talked about all the steps Toyota had taken so that errors would be stopped in their tracks; or how workers' suggestions were taken almost immediately into account; or how every method on the factory floor was subject to constant improvement.

And little wonder. At that time, Detroit auto plants were individual kingdoms, run by plant managers that had the ultimate say over the methods used on the assembly line floor. Factories were mazes of duplication and waste, with weeks of parts kept stashed away in case of an unexpected strike by workers somewhere in the pipeline that cut off supplies. The concept of a company that used the same ideas and practices in each of its factories, and that made a conscious effort to limit its inventory of auto parts, was as foreign as Cho's native tongue. To put it bluntly, nobody really got it—and for Toyota, that was just as well.

But Cho had more on his mind than simply explaining the Toyota precepts to a group of American engineers; the ultimate goal was to eliminate the shroud of mystery that had so long colored Americans' perception of the company. He wanted to make Toyota seem more approachable, because the company knew that, sooner or later, it was going to venture out into the world and would need all the friends and supporters it could get.

Its image was indeed in need of revamping. At the time, Detroit was deep in a recession whose overtones foreshadowed the crisis that would grip the industry a quarter-century later. Chrysler had been forced to seek a congressional bailout plan, and GM and Ford were battling their own financial woes (only the profits from Ford's international operations were helping to stave off its own federal bailout request). Protectionist rhetoric was reaching a crescendo, as critics assailed Japanese companies, blaming them for Detroit's woes and accusing them of using less-expensive labor at home to flood the American market with cheap cars. Fearing the backlash would cost the company access to the most important market in the world, Cho knew he had to go public with what it was doing in its factories and convince Americans that there was more to Toyota than just exploitation of cheap parts and labor—in other words, convince them that the company "wasn't as bad as people think," Cho told me during our interview in Nagoya. "[I knew] we could not go back to what we were in the past. We have to keep up our efforts so that we can be accepted by the people over there."

By introducing America to Toyota's methods, Cho began to chip away at the mental barrier that many Americans had erected between homegrown and foreign entities. In removing the shroud covering the carmaker, he helped the American public to stop seeing Toyota as a malevolent interloper but instead as a friendly—if still somewhat elusive—guest who might someday be allowed to put down roots in our country. "Personally, I would be very happy if Toyota was viewed as an American company," Cho said, pouring cream into a cup of strong coffee. "That way of viewing Toyota is a favorable view." To this day, he believes that the work he did to win over the American public had paid off. Cho knows that for all its systems, the company's story comes across better when told in human terms. "The most critical factor [to Toyota's success]," he said, "will be people," And he is right.

WATANADE: MASTERMIND—AND RESCUE ARTIST

Near the headquarters where Cho sat, another new tower recently rose at the manufacturing center in Toyota City, about thirty miles west from Nagoya. For decades, Toyota had made do with a modest, unremarkable headquarters, a squat low-rise that sat amid the buildings that stretch for miles like the Japanese equivalent of the Rouge complex in Dearborn, Michigan. A lone bust of Kiichiro Toyoda, the company's founder, sitting at the foot of the driveway leading to the building was the sole sign announcing to outside visitors that this was where Toyota's brain trust sat. Now, that same statue, covered in verdigris, stands outside an imposing glass and steel skyscraper that has served as the company's global manufacturing nerve center since 2005.

The new Toyota City building has much more in common with the new offices in Nagoya than with its predecessor, which is now used primarily for storage. It has a restaurant in the basement and tastefully decorated hallways in modern Asian style. When visitors arrive, they are greeted and escorted up to the thirteenth floor, where reception rooms are decorated with groups of low leather chairs and meeting tables. Windows look out on a vast sea of other buildings that have been constructed just in the past few years, including a design center, an engineering center, and a welcome center called the Toyota Kaikan, where half a million visitors—businesspeople and vacationers alike—converge each year.

The main draw for visitors is the chance to tour Toyota's factories, such as Tsutsumi, home to the hybrid-electric Prius. There they can stroll through the numerous displays showcasing Toyota's advancements in environmental technology; there is a cutaway version of the Prius, a primer on hydrogen fuel cells, and a large showroom that allows guests to kick the tires of Toyotas built around the world. In one auditorium, a group of robots plays music to an appreciative audience. (I spent most of my time trying to figure out if the robots were just playing along to a recording, but they were actually blowing trumpets and other instruments, playing tunes such as "Take the A Train.") It is a playful display meant to illustrate the company's position as a leader in the field of robotics—on the factory floor, of course, where robots are used to move parts and streamline operations, not provide musical accompaniment.

It is at the new Toyota city building, too, that Toyota showcases its global bent; in one of the exhibit rooms, a large mural displays the flags of every Toyota operation around the world, while a bulletin board features pictures of myriad Toyota employees—American, Brazilian, Chinese, European, and Japanese—presumably to advertise the company's diversity.

Until the summer of 2009, the man in charge of all this was Katsuaki Watanabe, who, like Cho, readily credits the company's American employees, factories, and dealers for making Toyota the global operation it has become. There were no great expectations for Watanabe when he was named president in 2005, succeeding Cho. Born in 1942 and trained as an economist, he had previously run the company's research and development arm as well as its global public affairs, and he had never held a position outside Japan. His only manufacturing experience was as supervisor of the Motomachi plant, and he had never been in charge of developing any specific Toyota models. His role, when he was appointed to the president's job, seemed to be less that of a leader and more that of caretaker.

When Cho stepped down in the middle of the decade, many company observers assumed Toyota would name Akio Toyoda, Kiichiro's grandson, as its next president. But the lengthy apprenticeship that had been devised for Toyoda was not yet complete, and observers said Watanabe, the quintessential insider, would do in the interim. "Mr. Watanabe is a transitional CEO, standing in before Mr. Toyoda can take the helm," said Hirofumi Yokoi, a former Toyota accountant who is an analyst at CSM Worldwide, an auto industry research company. "Mr. Watanabe will be easy to replace when the time comes."

It did not turn out to be that simple. Instead, Watanabe, who far exceeded the expectations company officials had for him, will go down in the annals of Toyota as its first truly global president. By building on the expansion begun by Shoichiro Toyoda, the aggressive moves by Hiroshi Okuda, and the inroads made by Fujio Cho, and leveraging what Toyota has learned in the United States, he grew the company into not just a large Japanese player, but also a global one—one that manufactures vehicles in 27 countries, owns 53 subsidiaries, and sells vehicles in 163 nations. If Cho can be credited with taking the first step to demystify Toyota and turn it into the equivalent of an American company, it is Watanabe (whose English is much better than he likes to let on) who picked up where he left off— and charged full steam ahead. Under his tenure Toyota's U.S. market share swelled from about 10 percent in 2005 to 17 percent in 2009, passing first Chrysler and then Ford, to rank as the second biggest player in the American market, essentially rendering the phrase "the Big Three" obsolete.

But as he has come to grips with Toyota's growth in the United States, where until late this decade the company was on a nearly uninterrupted path of steady expansion, he has faced greater challenges—and greater public scrutiny—than perhaps any other executive in the company's history. As the man who steered the company ahead of the American automakers, in some circles he is held partly responsible for Detroit's demise; even within the company, he has found himself criticized for being too aggressive and ambitious in his plans for U.S. growth (never mind the fact that it was Toyota's American operations that provided the seed for its global expansion and record profits). "I do believe he faced the toughest job of any Toyota CEO, ever," said John Casesa, the automobile industry analyst. Not only did Watanabe have to deal with Toyota's new high-profile reality, he also faced "the prospect of remaking this company to deal with emerging competition, the green revolution, and the prospects of slower growth." Indeed, as we will read later, many analysts laid blame at Watanabe's feet for the company's massive 2008 loss, its first since 1950, and the prospect that it would lose even more after the company's deep financial crisis ended.

Watanabe has also had to wrestle with another major challenge to Toyota's reputation in the United States. For decades, Toyota had long relied on its record, shared with Honda, of building the best automobiles in the world. Year after year, cars and trucks from Toyota ranked at or near the top of quality surveys, and Toyota's name has been renowned throughout manufacturing circles for its focus on quality and on continuous improvement. It has always been several frustrating paces ahead of Detroit auto companies, who could never claim a record as solid as that of Toyota's, no matter how much they insisted their cars were every bit as good.

"They're good. They're the New England Patriots," said a

former senior executive at a Detroit company. "The bottom line is that they are giving customers what they want, all over the world. There is no variability on Toyota cars." But even Toyota, it turned out, was vulnerable to quality problems, and when it stumbled, the whole world took notice. In 2005, when it was forced to recall two million vehicles, Watanabe found himself in a public relations nightmare. Because the company was growing and expanding so rapidly around the world, its legendary lean processes simply weren't enough to shield it from the quality control problems that plagued other car companies. Moreover, it could not get the word out fast enough that improvements needed to be made. "When Toyota was a small company, we could expressly communicate" any quality improvements that were required. "But now that Toyota is so big, we've realized that we have not adequately communicated," he said during the 2008 Detroit Auto Show. So Watanabe did what no American executive and few Japanese executives would do—he bowed low to the media and publicly apologized for the defects.

"We've been facing tough questions from our customers who became anxious about their cars' safety. We deeply apologize to them," Watanabe said. It was a move so uncharacteristic for a Japanese executive of his stature that it caused a buzz throughout the automotive world. Apologies themselves were not entirely unheard of in Japanese companies, where managers in the most extreme cases might commit suicide in the face of a corporate scandal. But in a country where rank is the ultimate determinant of authority, Watanabe was the level of executive to whom others bowed deeply, not the other way around.

Some of Toyota's American managers were appalled by Watanabe's action, viewing it as unnecessary groveling by such an important leader, but his move worked wonders in winning back consumers' trust. In a single moment, the bow shattered the perception of Watanabe as an anonymous administrator and made industry experts take a closer look at his managerial acumen and public relations savvy. "Many assumed he would be a weak transitional player," said Takaki Nakanishi, an analyst in Tokyo for J.P. Morgan Securities. "But he has surprised everyone."

Watanabe said the incident taught him a key lesson about the need to juggle the different requirements of the many markets where Toyota operates. "If we really force the way we do work in Japan and try to transplant the way of work to all the countries in the world, we would end up in failure," he told me. "In order to come up with the best product for the U.S., first of all there has to be the common understanding of the Toyota Way, which is universal, and then have the American people work on what would be best for the United States, and construct this U.S. best practice and U.S. best methodology on their own. This is the kind of localization that I want to promote."

In other words, he realized that to become a successful global player, Toyota would have to carve a role for itself in American society. He went on, "As we have initiated our global operation and especially since we have made inroads in the U.S. market . . . we had a gradual change in our mindset with regards to how we see the world," he said. "We have realized a global vision is very important. At the same time, Toyota had to be aware about what people were saying about it, and be sensitive to all kinds of developments." Toyota also must "be privy to the political situation, the economic situation, and the social situation in each region in order to have a global operation." Watanabe knew Toyota could not wear blinders. "It's really taken for granted that the sentiment of the Japanese is not the same as the sentiment of colleagues in the United States. This is driven by ethnicity and difference in tradition," he said.

"So of course, the American peers would always have in mind, to what extent would Toyota trust us? To what extent would they delegate to us? I want very good, smooth global communication to take place."

Watanabe would soon have bigger worries than Toyota's PR problems. In late 2008 it became clear that Toyota was not shielded from the economic forces that roiled the rest of the economic world, and Watanabe found himself facing the deepest financial crisis that Toyota had encountered since its founding years. Its global sales plunged. After years of record profits, which had given Toyota a market capitalization of nearly $200 billion, the company ended 2008 with its first net loss—nearly $4 billion—since 1950, and its first operating loss since Kiichiro Toyoda began building cars in 1937. The situation became known inside the company as "the emergency" and came as a shock to both insiders and students of the company, who found it hard to believe that Toyota, which had earned a record profit of nearly $20 billion two years earlier, could have fallen so far so fast.

Only two years after Watanabe had traveled to Texas to dedicate the company's latest assembly plant, Toyota was forced to cut its production, temporarily shut down both its San Antonio factory and its plant in Princeton, Indiana, and delay the start of production at Blue Springs, Mississippi until sometime in the next decade. By Christmas 2008, Watanabe's job was on the line, and in a bold move, Toyota decided that the time had come for Akio Toyoda to take the stage.

AMERICAN-TRAINED FAMILY SCION

At home, Akio Toyoda is an A-list celebrity. In the years before he was promoted to president, he could not make one of his rare appearances at an auto show or a company event without being mobbed by journalists thrusting microphones and tape recorders at him from every angle like paparazzi on Sunset Boulevard. (Presumably, he will be surrounded by security now that he has the top job.) But despite his outsized popularity in his home country, in the United States, Toyoda preferred to keep a low and modest profile. Even as recently as April 2009, just weeks before his promotion to chief executive, he was able to make a stealth visit to Washington without attracting public attention, something no CEO from one of the beleaguered Detroit companies would be able to do. Though fluent in English, Toyoda was consistently kept away from Western journalists, leaving the American public wondering: Who is the real Akio Toyoda?

The answer is complicated. He is a member of one of the most famous business families in Japan and the assumed heir to one of the country's biggest corporate empires. Yet he went to America to earn his MBA, and he stayed out of Toyota until he was twenty-eight—years after most trainees join the company. He is the first Toyota president to have been both trained and educated in the United States, and the first to embody such a unique hybrid of the two cultures. He has managed to seamlessly integrate his Japanese upbringing with his later-acquired American sensibilities, and to remain both a respected representative of his family and an ordinary baby boomer who gave me one of the most relaxed interviews I have ever experienced with a Japanese executive.

After earning an undergraduate degree in law from Keio University in Tokyo (the same school Watanabe attended), Toyoda traveled to Massachusetts to earn his MBA at Babson, where all the classes were taught in English. At first, Toyoda missed the familiar routine of his home country and struggled to keep up with his classes. It was one thing to speak English fluently and quite another to study in it, he found. "That was a tough three years," said Toyoda. But he soon acclimated, and upon graduation, he didn't immediately return home to take a job at the family company; he remained in the United States and took a job as an investment banker in New York with A. G. Becker, living in a co-op apartment just off Fifth Avenue at 3 East Seventy-first Street, next door to the Frick Collection.

At Becker he was part of a team of ten associates, including six women, one of whom was his supervisor. "At a company like Toyota, I would have never experienced a lady boss," he said, laughing. Like many young managers in the 1980s, when it was far trendier to deal with a flock of companies, not just one, Toyoda eventually decided he would prefer to explore the consulting world, and he wound up at Booz Allen Hamilton. There, he came face-to-face with his family heritage. For the first time in his career, he said, his colleagues regularly brought up Toyota and began to ask him about his future association with the company. He hardly knew how to answer.

Unlike in Japan, where his name conferred an assumed knowledge about anything automotive, at Booz Allen Hamilton, he did not handle projects dealing with the car industry; when a superior assigned him to an auto industry project, incorrectly assuming that his family ties qualified him for the task, Toyoda stepped back for a personal reassessment. "People look at me and think I am an expert in the automobile industry, and I'm not," he said. It was just one of a number of revelations that caught me off guard.

In 2008, I finally had the chance to meet the elusive young Toyoda, after years of deflected requests for an interview. In hindsight, Toyota's decision to make him available was probably one more calculated step in his grooming for the top job. Actually, I hadn't expected to see him at all during my trip to Japan, and I was hoping to spend a few minutes with his father, Shoichiro Toyoda, the company's honorary chairman. But to my pleasant surprise, I was instead awarded what was originally described as a fifteen-minute courtesy call (or meet and greet, in Washington terms) with his son.

Even after I arrived for the meeting, I was told that Toyoda did not want to sit through a long interview, and under no circumstances would he agree to a photograph. So, primed for a scripted and brief interview with an executive who would stay on message the entire time, I was surprised when the usual formalities of a Japanese interview were quickly dispensed with. During an hour-long conversation conducted almost entirely in English, Toyoda cracked jokes, told stories, and, midway through the interview, even allowed photographer Ayumi Nakanishi to snap his picture. (He struck us both as something of a dandy. While in New York, he picked up a sense for fashion, and he arrived for the interview in a stylish gray pinstriped suit with a checked shirt and heliotrope tie instead of the usual Japanese uniform of dark business attire. On the day he was named president, he was sporting a striking lavender tie.)

Instead of the usual exchange of business cards, small talk, and less-than-revealing answers, Toyoda showed up with a DVD player queued up to play a recording of the June 2007 Nürburgring race, the twenty-four-hour race at Germany's famous track, in which he had participated as a driver for the Toyota team. As we chatted, I watched almost in disbelief as Toyoda, coached by the team's chief driver, took a modified Lexus 300 through the twisting curves of the ring's 3.2-mile course, cruising at 150 mph down its straightaway, shifting down to speeds of no less than 108 mph. It would be one thing for a race car driver to pull that off—and an entirely different thing for a nonprofessional to do.

Toyoda's participation in the grueling annual race was far more than a testament to his concentration and endurance; it was his way of showing that he was committed and willing to take on the top job to which most in the company assumed he would ascend—but that he would do this job *his* way. "For the youthful Akio to go near a race track is one thing," journalist Peter Nunn wrote on the *Winding Road*, a Web-based car magazine. "To race in the bruising, madcap 'Ring 24 Hours is something else again . . . something few Japanese execs would even dream of contemplating."

During his last hour on the road, tears were running down his cheeks, Toyoda recalled. They came not just from the stress of the event, which might have been reason enough, but also from the realization that he had finally reached another milestone in his quest to understand his grandfather's auto company.

Over the previous ten years, he had gone out on the company's test track one day a month, driving Toyota's entire lineup, as well as cars from its competitors, one model at a time, trying to get a sense of what made the cars—and the company—tick. Still, as a non-engineer, it eluded him. So he had decided to take on the racing training at the behest of the company's test drivers who felt it would help Toyoda, who had received his driver's license in the United States, to get a better understanding of the company's vehicles. "The chief driver told me, 'If you don't know how to drive the vehicles, we can't do our work,' " Toyoda said. (He sometimes jokes about his lack of product development expertise. Asked whether he wished he had become an engineer, he answered, "No, no, no, I'm not smart enough.")

To the young executive, this understanding was critical. "If I am going to be at the top of the car company, I want to be the owner-chef"—meaning a restaurant owner who not only runs his business but also prepares every dish served to diners—he said. A revered profession in Japan, the owner-chef is considered to be the ultimate expert on a restaurant's offerings, and Toyoda made clear that he used the term deliberately. "I taste my car, and if it tastes good, I provide it to the customer," he went on.

Running Toyota might seem to be his birthright, but it was never a sure thing. "Whether Akio gets the top job depends on circumstances, not on some inevitability in the return of a Toyoda," said James P. Womack. But the circumstances aligned and in January 2009, Toyota announced that Toyoda would get the job the following June. The financial crisis aside, senior executives had two theories why the Toyota family, which still had incredible influence in the company even though they held only a few percent of its stock, decided to push Watanabe aside and install Toyoda. One was that his father, Shoichiro, was still in good health and wanted his son to run the company while he would be lucid enough to advise him. The other was that the elder Toyoda wanted his son to have the experience of managing in a downturn, as well as the reputational benefit of steering it through recovery.

But Akio's father had never once guaranteed him that the job would be his. On a visit home from New York in 1984, when the young Toyoda asked Shoichiro whether he should join the family company, he received a less than enthusiastic response. "Nobody wants to be your boss," the elder Toyoda said. "Toyota doesn't need you. If you want to work here, just follow the normal way," meaning to start as a management trainee. So, that fall, at twenty-eight, Toyoda joined the company as the oldest trainee in a class made up primarily of recent college graduates. Training complete, he began his Toyota career just like any other young prospect, spending three months working on the assembly line at the Motomachi plant and three months working in a car dealership.

Then his real training began in earnest. One of his first assignments was at Toyota's joint venture plant with GM in California, known as NUMMI, where he was in charge of production control. His responsibilities were not significant; it was primarily an opportunity to listen and learn, especially in how to work with the Americans that GM sent there. Although the joint venture was a signature move by his father, Shoichiro Toyoda offered him little guidance, then or ever, on how to manage his career. "He doesn't influence me," Akio said of his father. But Toyoda seems remarkably sanguine about it, theorizing that his father's hands-off attitude stems from losing his own father, Kiichiro, in 1952, when he was only twenty-seven. "He didn't have a father at my age," Akio said, and there was no template for Shoichiro to follow in his dealings with an employee son.

Thus it was through a combination of hard work, dedication, and business acumen—rather than special treatment or guidance from his family—that Toyoda climbed up the ranks of the company, one step at a time. In doing so, Toyoda took a different path than Watanabe, and one that more closely echoed that of Fujio Cho. Along with his assignment in America, he ran Toyota's operations in China, and then was put in charge of its Japanese and ultimately its North American operations.

Along the way, he took time out to do things no president before him would have dreamed of. For one, he launched a Web site, Gazoo.com, that was aimed at convincing young consumers to consider Toyota's used cars. Within a few years, it had grown to become a social network as well, with restaurant reviews, message boards, and, of course, ads from Toyota. By the time he was named president, his résumé looked nothing like that of a typical Japanese executive, but very much like one of a twenty-first-century American CEO.

Though he has now risen to the top job, he still retains his modest U.S. persona. In fall 2008, I was surprised to learn that Toyoda had made a stop at the dealership in Ann Arbor, Michigan, where I had bought my Prius (the subject of my blog, the Prius Diary, on the *New York Times'* Green, Inc., Web page). While he was there, he asked to see one of the Toyota Tacoma pickup trucks that the company had recalled for corrosion. Getting down on his hands and knees on the warm blacktop, he took a look under the car, shocking his American hosts, who never thought they would see the future president of their company taking such a close inspection.

Perhaps his hands-on style is the result of spending much of his career in the awkward position of son and subordinate. "I respect my father as a father, but I also respect him as an honorable chairman," Toyoda said, choosing his words carefully. Taking such a different career path from that of the generations of Toyodas before him gave him "the freedom and the chance to think by myself, which is good for a person like me to do."

Asked whether he felt any personal ambiguity over the prospect of running such a global giant, Toyoda said he would have plenty of assistance. "I'm not alone. I'm not the only one," he said, smiling. Indeed, on the day his appointment was announced, Toyoda walked into a crowded news conference accompanied by Watanabe on his left and Cho on his right. Cho looked proud, and Watanabe had a broad smile, perhaps of relief that the difficulties he had been forced to tackle in his final months would be handed off to someone else. At the news conference that followed, Toyoda appeared completely aware of what had been thrust upon him. "I have assumed the huge responsibility of steering Toyota at a time when we're facing a once-in-a-century crisis," he said. "Given the circumstances, I take my responsibility very seriously."

To prove this point, he vowed to "go to the spot" as he did in Ann Arbor, to see every part of Toyota for himself. That is likely to mean more trips to the United States, where Watanabe, despite his aggressive U.S. strategy, ventured only a few times during his tenure. When he visits, he now should prepare himself for a Brad Pitt–style reception. A young, dynamic president, trained and educated in New York and Boston; fluent in

English; stylish; cosmopolitan; enthusiastic about racing; and familiar with the company's operations in its three biggest markets—America, Japan, and China—is guaranteed to attract an unprecedented amount of attention.

If nothing else, the company's decision to entrust him with this role sends an unequivocal signal to the American public that Toyota is ready to be seen as a new kind of global company. The next years will show whether the young Toyoda's American-Japanese sensibility is right for the job. In the meantime, he is likely to undergo incredible scrutiny, both as a Toyoda and as the president of the world's largest car company working to dig itself out of a global crisis. If his promise pays off, he could well become one of the powerful and influential executives in the world.

One thing is for certain, though. Toyoda will be a visible symbol of everything that Toyota wants to become. After just a few months at the helm, he had already spent time in Washington, cultivating political leaders such as Jay Rockefeller, and all signs indicate that he will carry on the company's commitment to sizable U.S. investment. There is no other foreign company that has played the role in the U.S. economy that Toyota has, and its future here will be a barometer and an example for other companies in the difficult years ahead.

Toyoda, at least, seems ready for his moment. Leaving our interview, he skipped the ceremonial bows that normally end a meeting in Japan, and came over to exchange a warm handshake. "Next time," he said, making an offer I would never refuse, "I'll drive you."

Chapter Ten

THE NEW FACE
OF THE
AMERICAN ECONOMY

Your own safety is at stake when your neighbor's house is ablaze.

—HORACE

I mages have a way of freezing a moment in time. No photographer did more to document the yawning gap between the haves and have-nots than Arthur Felig (better known by his nickname, Weegee) with his iconic 1943 picture of a homeless woman gazing at two opera-going women in tiaras and furs. In the 1970s, nothing depicted the desperate hours of the oil crisis than the photo of acres and acres of unsold Chryslers parked on the Michigan State Fairgrounds, not a buyer in sight.

In the fall of 2008, one image captured the desperate irony of a time when widespread economic collapse brought many of the nation's biggest, boldest, and, at one time, most profitable and powerful institutions to their knees. The now infamous photo, taken during a congressional hearing for the auto bailout, depicted the sea of icy stares that met Brad Sherman, a Democratic representative from California, when he asked the chief executives of GM, Ford, and Chrysler to "raise their hand if they flew here commercial." Not a hand went up among the executives, because each had traveled to Washington to beg for $17 billion in government aid on their private corporate jets.

America's immediate, indignant, and even vitriolic reaction to this image, which was soon plastered across newspapers and the blogosphere, looped over and over on cable and network news, and lampooned mercilessly on the talk shows and immortalized as the new face of corporate America's greed and excess, demonstrated just how far the mighty had fallen—not just in their stock price, but in the esteem of the American public (not to mention onlookers all over the world).

In early 2009, another image was flying in Washington: that of the American flag. As Democrats scurried to put together the $787 billion stimulus package, sought by President Obama, lawmakers sympathetic to labor interests slipped in a "Buy American" provision requiring that any infrastructure projects launched by the government be required to use American-made steel, textiles, and other building materials. This step, which came as Timothy Geithner, in confirmation hearings on his nomination to become Treasury secretary, made an offhand comment accusing China of manipulating its currency, could only mean one thing: Once again (and perhaps not surprisingly given the dismal condition of the economy), protectionist rhetoric was alive and well in Washington. The only way to save American jobs, proponents of the provision insisted, in tones that starkly echoed those of the Great Depression, was to "Buy American."

The automakers, the "Buy American" proponents, and even Geithner soon learned, however, after an outcry from both within the administration and from governments abroad prompted the

Senate to hastily dilute although not delete the provision, that the American Dream was no longer a matter of red, white, and blue. It had become a rainbow, with colorful flags from all over the world bleeding together.

In hard times, the temptation to retreat into the comfortable shell of protectionism and economic nationalism is undeniably great. But the vehement public and political backlash against both the auto industry bailout and the "Buy American" proposal reflected difficulties in making such rhetoric stick. Finally, it seemed the nation had come to realize that protecting the American economy couldn't be done by picking sides or closing doors or pointing fingers. America, and its businesses, had become too much a part of the world at large. In order for the global economy to withstand the brunt of the economic downturn, it was clear that America had to remain open and willing to, participate in it.

HOW TO FIX A FLAT

More than any recent event in Congress, the 2008 auto bailout hearings brought into sharp focus how easily an industry—perhaps the most American of industries—can lose its cherished place in the economy and in American hearts and minds. As shocked as Detroit industry leaders were to be asked about the use of their private planes, they were even more stunned to experience the hail of venom that rained down on them as they pleaded for federal aid. It wasn't just that Americans had turned their backs on their automobiles (Detroit's grip on the car market had long been loosened by foreign competition); Americans were turning their backs on their business practices, their principles, and even—as evidenced by a CBS News poll reporting that 44 percent of Americans disapproved of the bailout package without which GM and Chrysler seemed likely to go bankrupt—their very existences.

In turning away from their homegrown fixtures, Americans simultaneously were turning their eyes toward the foreign—indeed, the only—alternatives. Case in point: By the time 2008 drew to a close, Detroit's share of the American car market had slipped below 50 percent, giving foreign companies the upper hand for the first time. This shift toward foreign players wasn't confined to the marketplace, nor was it just a shift in public opinion. This fall from favor even among those who had once championed their interests was being mirrored in Washington as well—a fact that became abundantly clear when the companies went to Congress in search of support. As Congress again and again refused the automakers' pleas for help (later granted in the last weeks of the Bush administration), a new phrase was born: the "Toyota Republicans." Led by a Tennessee senator, Bob Corker, the Toyota Republicans were a powerful group of largely southern lawmakers (though not all Republicans, and not all southerners) who, sharply critical of Detroit companies for failing to compete with foreign automakers on their own soil, vehemently opposed the bailout legislation and lobbied heavily to keep it from making its way through Congress.

What's more, Detroit companies had not only lost the support of their base in Congress, they could not even count on the support of their own trade group, the Alliance of Automobile Manufacturers, which failed to lead a rally behind them on the subject of the bailout. In a sign of how much had changed, it seemed that the Detroit companies no longer had enough clout to make even their own lobbying group come to their assistance.

This wasn't Detroit's only PR problem. For weeks, prominent message boards and blogs—including those posted on the *New York Times* Web site—were flooded with messages unsympathetic to the plight of the American carmakers. "If and when they do have to bury Detroit, I hope that all the current and past representatives and senators from Michigan have to serve as pallbearers," *Times* columnist Thomas Friedman wrote in "How to Fix a Flat," a column published in December 2008.

As the battle of words took place, Detroit companies desperately sought support from any source they could find. They resorted to pleas, patriotism, and ultimately scare tactics, warning that as many as three million American jobs might be lost if one of them went out of business, posing a serious threat to middle-class way of life (not mentioning that an entirely new auto industry had risen in the past twenty years to offset some of the jobs that they had eliminated).

All of this made for a lively, albeit heated, debate in Washington and across the nation, but in the end these pleas fell on deaf ears; none were enough to convince the Toyota Republicans in the U.S. Senate to support legislation that had been passed by the House of Representatives. The message was clear: Three of the oldest and most iconic American companies were one sharp blow to the head away from death, and most of the nation didn't care—and why should they, so many reasoned, when Toyota, Honda, and the like were ready and willing to step in and take Detroit's place? Foreign companies had spent the past two decades courting American consumers—the same consumers Detroit had managed to alienate—making them feel satisfied with their products and comfortable with their American presence, and it had paid off. Eventually, the Bush administration issued the carmakers a lifeline, and the Obama administration followed suit, coming to their rescue with billions more in assistance, plus the tough love of a forced bankruptcy filing. But the American public had finally woken up to the fact that American companies—not just in the auto industry but in all sectors of the economy—were no longer the only game in town.

THE RETURN OF "BUY AMERICAN"

In January 2009, as the newly appointed members of the Obama cabinet began to populate the offices of the West Wing, the phrase "Buy American" once again began to reverberate through the halls of Congress, on radio and television airwaves, and in union halls nationwide. This was because the stimulus package that President Obama so fervently sought to jump-start the ailing economy and create as many as three million jobs through a series of public works projects across the country contained a provision, pushed by lobbyists for the steel industry and major labor organizations such as the AFL-CIO, requiring that these new projects give preference to American-made steel, textiles, uniforms, and other products. "Buying American steel is a smart use of taxpayer dollars that will create American jobs and enable us to build a stronger, safer United States," said Pete Visclosky, a Democratic congressman whose northern Indiana district included a variety of steel makers. Although the "Buy American" provision applied to all American-*made* goods, regardless of where the company was owned or based (in other words, it didn't specifically discriminate against goods made in American plants owned by foreign companies), the primary goal of the measure was clear—to use trade restraint as a tool to shore up American companies.

Sending a message redolent of George W. Bush's now-famous response when asked what Americans could do to help their country after 9/11 (essentially, go shopping), it seemed as if consumers were being promised they could solve all the country's economic woes merely by purchasing American-made goods. But the solution, as its proponents soon realized, was not that simple.

The "Buy American" provision quickly ignited concern in Europe (leaders spent hours during the World Economic Forum in Davos, Switzerland, denouncing the idea), and for good reason. Peter Power, a spokesman for the European Union, said the measure sent "the worst possible signal," and would sour relations between the United States and the rest of the world. John Bruton, the EU's representative to the United States, said the measure, if passed, could erode global leadership on free trade, with huge consequences for all the major economic players, America included. "We regard this legislation as setting a very dangerous precedent at a time when the world is facing a global economic crisis," Bruton said. After all, once the government starts dictating where goods can be produced, the slope becomes incredibly slippery, many critics of the provision rightly reasoned, for who is to say that the next time, the requirement won't be goods produced by a company with 75 percent American ownership or goods produced by a company based in south-central Indiana? As Syed Kamall, a spokesman for the European Parliament's

Conservative Party warned, "Buy American" restrictions could lead to an "economic iron curtain."

The Europeans weren't the only ones who were upset: Canada, which has long been America's biggest trading partner, and which shipped $11 billion a year in steel to American customers, understandably found the provision alarming, as well. Stephen Harper, Canada's prime minister, said the clause threatened all industrialized countries, not just the United States. "These are not measures targeted at Canada; they are measures that are of concern to all trading partners of the United States," Harper said. As the representatives of the G20 nations agreed when they met in Washington in late 2008, as the scope of the global damage wreaked by the subprime crisis was just being realized, a solution that was designed to help only, or even primarily, American companies would end up helping no one at all. "We had to have a global response to the recession, which would include stimulus packages in all major countries and the avoidance of protectionism . . . in a stimulus package," Harper said.

There were myriads of concerns within our borders, too. American companies with extensive operations overseas, such as General Electric and Caterpillar, as well as the U.S. Chamber of Commerce, quickly spoke out against the provision, for fear that it would hurt their chances of doing business outside the United States; after all, such brazenly protectionist policies would almost certainly, as Treasury Secretary Geithner cautioned, incite retaliatory measures by our trading partners. "Protectionism will do little to create jobs, and if foreigners retaliate, we surely will lose jobs," concurred Alan Greenspan, the former Federal Reserve chairman. And it's not just American companies that would pay the price of such measures; tomorrow's workers and taxpayers would eventually suffer, too, saddled by the debt incurred by a less efficient and productive economy as well as higher tariffs and prices. Closing doors to foreign trade, in the words of Secretary Geithner, simply "doesn't make economic sense."

History has time and again shown us that protectionism moves us economically backward, not ahead. As the *Economist* warned in an editorial, if Obama did not nip the provision in the bud, we could find ourselves in a situation rivaling the 1930s, when the passage of the Hawley-Smoot Tariff Act exacerbated the Great Depression by raising the price of foreign goods. "If there is one thing we know for absolute certain, it's this," concurred Thomas Friedman in his February 11, 2009, column in the *New York Times*. "Protectionism did not cause the Great Depression, but it sure helped to make it 'Great.' From 1929 to 1934, world trade plunged by more than 60 percent—and we were all worse off. We live in a technological age where every study shows that the more knowledge you have as a worker and the more knowledge workers you have as an economy, the faster your incomes will rise. Therefore, the centerpiece of our stimulus, the core driving principle, should be to stimulate everything that makes us smarter and attracts more smart people to our shores. That is the best way to create good jobs."

One can't even begin to contemplate the costs of the diplomatic fallout from passing the original "Buy American" provision—especially at a time when President Obama was just beginning to repair relationships with leaders of other governments after years of strain with the Bush administration. He moved swiftly to caution Congress. "We need to make sure that any provisions that are in there are not going to trigger a trade war," Obama said in a series of television interviews in early February 2009.

For these reasons and more, the "Buy American" clause ultimately was watered down to allow the heads of federal agencies to ignore the requirement if it would "be inconsistent with the public interest" or "applied in a manner inconsistent with United States obligations under international agreements." It was also stripped of certain restrictions likely to upset our trading partners, such as those covering infrastructure projects, including airports, railroads, and mass transit. (As the *New York Times* headline on February 19, 2009, said, "Good luck with that.") In fact, under the final version of the stimulus legislation, foreign-based firms operating in the United States—such as Bell Labs, the research arm of Alcatel-Lucent of France—were eligible to seek funds from the $787 package.

President Obama told Peter Mansbridge in an interview on the Canadian Broadcasting Corporation just after signing the stimulus bill into law, "My administration is committed to making sure that even as we take steps to strengthen the U.S. economy, that we are doing so in a way that actually over time will enhance the ability of trading partners, like Canada, to work within our boundaries." (Obama had a personal stake in maintaining good relations with Canada, since his favorite device, the BlackBerry, is made by a Canadian company, as Mansbridge reminded him.) Still, the very existence of the provision in the first place demonstrated the fact that when the United States found itself in trouble, the urge for economic nationalism was difficult to resist.

Only time will tell how the role foreign investment plays in our economy, in Washington, and in our society will change in the wake of the current meltdown. But whatever the future might bring for our economy, the fact remains that despite the wide reach of the global economic turmoil (at the time of this writing, the UK banking system is in crisis, Japan's economy is falling at the fastest rate since the oil crisis of the 1970s, and even the once unflappable Swiss are feeling the brunt of the downturn), foreign economies may be quicker than ours to fully recover—and when they do, their companies will be much more equipped to lend money than ever before. After all, think about how the picture of foreign investment has changed in just the past few decades; when the last worldwide recession hit, in 1982, Honda had only just completed its first American factory, and all the U.S. plants from Toyota, Nissan, Mercedes-Benz, and the other companies were yet to come. The aerospace and defense makers that eventually got together to become EADS were operating as separate companies with no U.S. presence and had no dreams of manufacturing steel or helicopters in Columbus, Mississippi. There was no hint that a British bank would buy up the detritus of a Wall Street powerhouse, or that the beer brewed in St. Louis would someday be brewed under the wing of a Belgian company.

In other words, today, foreign companies offer a lifeline that simply wasn't there in the past—but it won't save us unless we're willing to let it.

Now, more than ever, the United States and foreign nations have to work hand in hand to find solutions that can help restore the global economy and set the stage for further growth. There is no question that as the nation grapples with and hopefully begins to come out of the crisis that has gripped its housing market, financial institutions, and manufacturing, media, and service industries, the need for outside investment has never been greater. We need now, more than ever, the involvement of more foreign investors such as Barclays (which bought the investment banking division of Lehman Brothers), Fiat (which took management control of Chrysler), Carlos Slim Helú (the Mexican mogul and part owner of the New York Times Company), Mitsubishi (whose $9 billion investment helped save Morgan Stanley), and others who have stepped in to pick up American companies' scattered remains. In these troubled times, recovery is not a matter of selling our economy *to* the world, but rather selling the world *on* our economy as a safe and desirable place to invest. We can only do so by showing foreign companies and their employees in the United States that they are welcome. Whatever protectionist rhetoric admittedly lingers, the new age of America—the America of Barack Obama—may finally be ready to do just that.

THE FUTURE OF FOREIGN INVESTMENT

The early decisions and policies steered by the Obama administration will be critical in shaping the role of foreign investment in the years ahead. The economic slowdown that began in 2007 (and deepened since) has demonstrated how investments by individuals and companies outside the United States can be invaluable in helping to both stabilize and stimulate the American economy. There is no question that foreign companies doing business in the United States would like to stay, and expand, once conditions improve. But with the real estate market in shambles and the banking and credit systems all but collapsed, whether America will remain an attractive place for foreign investors to do business in the years ahead is less certain. Whether these companies and investors forge ahead with their American operations or retreat back to their own shores will depend largely on how the new administration approaches the question of foreign investment.

I am confident that that foreign investment will continue to have a prominent role in the U.S. economy—perhaps an even more prominent and powerful one than it has had in the past eight years. In the months leading up to the November 2008 election, as it became clear to the world that Obama more or less had the presidential race clinched, many foreign companies began formulating plans to ramp up, and shift resources to, their U.S. operations, casting a clear vote of confidence that the new administration would not only repair the ailing economy, making the United States once again a profitable place to do business, but would also be sympathetic toward foreign interests. While Obama's campaign rhetoric evinced great concern for the plight of the American worker, he has never been seen, at home or abroad (where, unlike his predecessor, he is almost universally well regarded, in some cases even hailed as a celebrity of sorts), as a protectionist. During the presidential campaign he visited a number of plants and factories owned by foreign firms, including a wind-turbine manufacturing facility in Pennsylvania owned by the Spain-based Gamesa. As a senator of from Illinois, Obama represented a state that had long been friendly to foreign investors; in 2008 the state ranked sixth in the country in terms of jobs created by foreign companies.

Luckily, despite the huge losses sustained by the American economy in late 2008, and all the foreign outrage over the threat of protectionist provisions to the $787 billion stimulus package, in early 2009 many foreign companies still seemed to view the United States as a growth market. That February, the *New York Times* reported that a number of foreign entities based everywhere from Japan to France to South Korea were proceeding with plans to increase the volume of goods they would produce in the United States; this was good news for everyone, since this included plans to open new factories, plants, and offices—to be staffed primarily by Americans. For example, it was reported that Alstom, a French engineering company, was plunging ahead with its plans for a turbine factory in Tennessee, and that Sanyo remained committed to producing solar cells at its newly opened factory in Oregon and to opening a second American sales office in Dallas.

Much of this enthusiasm could be attributed to Obama's oft-stated commitment to the advancement of technologic and scientific research, especially clean energy, high-speed transit, and other green technologies. Indeed, his promise to "restore science to its rightful place" in Washington has been a clarion call to telecommunications, computing, and green energy businesses based overseas. This is why companies such as Alcatel-Lucent, a French telecom giant; Sanyo, the global maker of environment-related products; and Eurus Energy, a Japanese builder of wind farms, all announced, in late 2008, plans to expand their U.S. operations—a commitment they strengthened a few months later, once they learned that the stimulus package would invest $37.5 billion in energy, including $2.5 billion for energy efficiency and renewable-energy research and $6 billion for wind and solar. "With the new stimulus package that the federal government has announced, it is starting to appear that the U.S. market will be a prime location to focus much more effort on our environmental and energy-related technology and products," Sanyo spokesman Aaron S. Fowles told the *Washington Post* in March 2009.

To be sure, the global recession has forced foreign companies operating in the United States to stop and count every penny in every place they operate, both on our shores and around the world. Given that foreign companies have so much capacity outside the United States where costs are cheaper, if the American economy—and the American demand for goods—continues to suffer, will companies be tempted to shelve additional American production and simply ship goods from overseas? Or will they opt to push on with American production, taking advantage of the low costs of real estate, materials, and labor while hoping that demand for goods soon picks up, and that the new administration honors its commitment to economic, scientific, and technological growth while avoiding the temptation of protectionism and being mindful of foreign interests?

Most signs point to the latter. Still, by 2009, it couldn't be denied that, though the economic downturn was not hitting America as hard, relatively speaking, as some of its trading partners, America was becoming a less and less attractive place for foreign firms to invest—at least where the stock market was concerned. In 2008, the flow of foreign investment into American securities fell to just $412.5 billion, less than half the amount invested in 2007, and the lowest level since 1999. It was also the first year since 1987 that foreign investors were net sellers of stocks. Investors did not shy away from America completely, however; investments in Treasury bills soared to an unprecedented $456 billion. But those rock-solid investments carried little risk, since foreign investors could get their money out in a year if they did not like the direction their money, or the American economy, was taking.

While decisions about U.S. strategy will, of course, vary from investor to investor, company to company, and from sector to sector, one thing is certain: These decisions will be made with one eye toward the economy and the other toward political sentiment. No company knows the importance of this balance better than Toyota. "Toyota's DNA is one of paranoia," said George Borst, the veteran Toyota executive. "Politically, we want to make sure we're bringing in the right percentage of vehicles made in Japan versus American made."

Of any foreign company that does business in America, Toyota has arguably been the most visible and has enjoyed perhaps the most enviable period of success. As a result, the choices Toyota makes in the face of the economic downturn—how it climbs out of its sales decline, and whether it reroutes its ambitious plans for American production—may predict the path other global companies take in the American market as well.

Since the mid-1990s, Toyota has been on an unimpeded climb, in terms of market share. Even in 2008, when its sales fell along with many other automobile companies, Toyota saw its share of the American market reach 17 percent, only five points behind General Motors, putting it in second place among the country's carmakers. But slowed demand has prompted Toyota to put the breaks on some of its American production. Down in San Antonio, Texas, for example, sits a factory that is beginning to be viewed as a white elephant. Since opening in 2006, the $1.2 billion plant has never operated at peak production, and Toyota even shut the factory down for several months in 2008 and 2009 because the Tundra pickups built there could not find buyers.

San Antonio is not the only location affected by the slow-down. Toyota's next factory in Blue Springs, Mississippi, should have been open by now, but instead will not swing into full production until well into the next decade. This plant, which Haley Barbour so wanted for his state, and which was supposed to become the first factory outside Japan to build the Prius, is still years away from coming to fruition. A half-empty plant in Texas and an empty one in Mississippi are reminders that even Toyota is not immune to the market forces that hastened Detroit's demise.

Obviously, Toyota, as the most prominent foreign company in America, is at a fork in the road. Does it push forward as the most American of Japanese companies, a role it has to clearly and carefully establish for itself this decade? Or does it pull back closer to its Japanese roots and revert back to being the timid company that it was during its first forty years in the American car market? Akio Toyoda and other executives at the company may say there is no going back now, but at Toyota, actions always speak louder than its carefully considered words.

EADS also provides a useful lens through which to look at the future of foreign companies in America. It was dealt a significant blow when its ambitious plan to make a splash in the American market by landing the air force contract for refueling tanker planes was foiled in 2008, yet it hasn't let this setback derail either its ambitions nor its plans for U.S. expansion; in the coming years, it will be competing once more with Boeing to land the government's business as it presses toward a goal of $10 billion in annual revenues by 2020. Though less affected by the economic fallout than companies such as Toyota (after all, as long as we remain mired in Iraq and Afghanistan, the U.S. Air Force is unlikely to experience a steep drop in demand for tanker-refueling jets), EADS, like Toyota, has learned that public outcry can be an obstacle in its path. Is the contract more or less likely to be awarded under an Obama administration and a Democratic Congress? Will there be a compromise that will divide a deal between Airbus and Boeing, and assuage both northern Democrats and southern Republicans? Only time will tell. But one thing we can be sure of is that EADS now knows that when the next round of the tanker battle begins, it will have to create an atmosphere in Washington in which the Pentagon can feel comfortable awarding it.

A SALE WORTH MAKING

Clearly, the hundreds of foreign companies currently doing business in the United States have already been sold on the opportunities that the American economy provides. Companies such as Tata and Haier are eager, even anxious, to expand their presence here over the next decade. In order to attract such global investors in the future, however, particularly in these troubled economic times, our leaders will have to work hard to make them comfortable with the reception they will receive if they buy into their role in the American dream. This means that we, as a nation, will have to nip any nascent protectionist sentiment in the bud, coordinate our economic strategy with our trading partners, join other nations in encouraging open markets, and make sure that other developed countries continue to help nations still struggling to create viable economies. While foreign investment is vital to American workers, American communities, and the American economy, it isn't just our own future that hangs in the balance; one needs only to look at the reverberations our own banking crisis sent throughout the world to know that in today's global economy, as Madeline Albright famously said, "What matters anywhere matters everywhere."

How can we ensure a brighter future for not just our own companies, workers, and citizens, but those around the world? Donald Grimes, the University of Michigan economist, is among those who believe the answer lies in opening doors, not closing them. "I think people have learned from history," he said. "There's almost zero chance that we can go back to an isolationist position. And I think it's a good thing that we will avoid that. It's good for the economy, it's good for the culture, and it's good for the peace of the world." Protectionism only sets back the effort, for in the words of the John Legend song, "The future started yesterday, and we're already late."

In the end, companies such as Toyota, Tata, EADS, Haier, and all the others who have become part of the American fabric are here for the very same reasons that American companies invest overseas: They see an opportunity. As long as they, and others like them, adhere to American rules, obey American law, and respect their American workers, there is nothing for Americans to be afraid of. Of course, many people still fear that the American economy is up for sale, but in business, isn't buying and selling the only way for both parties to earn a profit? The profit that foreign companies are making is not theirs alone. It is being shared with American workers, American communities, and American society as a whole. That is a sale worth making.

Acknowledgments

T*he Selling of the American Economy* picks up where my last book, *The End of Detroit*, left off. But instead of explaining the demise of an industry, I wanted to write about the evolution of the American economy, thanks to the influence of foreign investment. My goal was to tell the story of American workers, communities, states, managers, executives, and government officials. As with *The End of Detroit*, I hope *The Selling of the American Economy* sparks a lively and much-needed discussion of an often-emotional situation. I understand how intensely personal the subject of foreign investment can be in America—but I also know there is more than one lens with which to view the result.

My thanks go first to my literary agent, Alice Fried Martell, and Roger Scholl, my editor at Broadway, for their unending faith in this project. I also want to thank my editors and colleagues at the *New York Times*, especially Larry Ingrassia, the editor of the Business Day section and Adam Bryant, the deputy editor, for their encouragement and support, especially during my years as bureau chief in Detroit, and throughout my *Times* career.

I received reporting assistance for this project from several *Times* contributors. Mickey Meece, formerly an editor at Business Day, conducted interviews in Georgetown and Lexington, Kentucky, and Princeton, Indiana. Kathryn Carlson and Mary M. Chapman provided reporting from New York and Detroit, respectively. I also thank

Acknowledgments

George Talbot at the *Mobile Press-Register* for his advice on understanding the South's approach to economic development.

At all of the companies that I profiled, my thanks go to the executives, managers, and team members around the world who agreed to interviews. At Toyota in the United States, I would like to thank Dennis Cuneo, Steve Curtis, Barbara McDaniel, Dan Sieger, Mike Goss, Carri Chandler, and Laquita Harris. In Japan, I thank Masami Doi, Osumu Goto, Yusei Higaki, Tomomi Imai, and especially Akiko Kita, for their assistance.

At EADS, I would like to thank Guy Hicks, Lawrence Stein, and Brenda Reuland. Thanks to Evan Goetz for his help with Tata, and James Liess at Haier. My thanks also go to my friend and fellow baseball fan David Barger at JetBlue Airways.

Thank you to the state and community leaders that I interviewed, particularly Governors Haley Barbour, Mitch Daniels, Jennifer M. Granholm, and Robert Riley, and U.S. senators Jay Rockefeller and Richard Shelby. I am grateful for the help I received from many experts, including John Casesa and Andrew Shapiro of the Casesa Shapiro Group, Gary Chaison at Clark University, Jeffrey Garten at Yale University, Jeffrey Liker and Donald Grimes at the University of Michigan, John Paul MacDuffie at the Wharton School, Matthew Slaughter at Dartmouth College, Mira Wilkins at Florida International University, and James P. Womack at the Lean Enterprise Institute. I also give special thanks to Michael Useem and his students at Wharton, and to mine at the University of Michigan's Ross School of Business.

Thank you, as always, to my family, and to all of my patient and supportive friends, especially Ian Austen, Bill Koenig, and Christine Tierney. Finally, to Douglas A. Fraser, I wish a hearty rest in peace with fond appreciation. I wish Doug could have gotten to read *The Selling of the American Economy* and given me another one of his priceless and insightful critiques.

References

The *Selling of the American Economy* is based primarily on hundreds of hours of original research, including interviews that I conducted exclusively for the book, along with my reporting as a senior business correspondent for the *New York Times*. Except as noted within the text and below, all direct quotes in the book are drawn from that research and from reporting assistance provided by Mickey Meece, Kathryn Carlson, and Mary M. Chapman, who are all *Times* contributors.

I conducted interviews and visited manufacturing plants in Michigan, Ohio, Indiana, Illinois, New York, Washington, D.C., West Virginia, Kentucky, Alabama, Mississippi, and Texas, as well as in Belgium, Canada, France, England, Germany, and Japan. In nearly all cases, those interviewed spoke on the record, but a few people requested anonymity, as specified in the book. The articles and books listed below were used primarily as background to supplement my reporting.

Introduction
Lindsey, Amy. Interview by Mickey Meece, 2007.

Chapter One: The Selling of the American Economy
McCain, John. Transcript of presidential debate. *New York Times*, September 26. 2008.

Wilkins, Mira. *The History of Foreign Investment in the United States to 1914.* Cambridge, Massachusetts: Harvard University Press, 1989.
———. *The History of Foreign Investment in the United States, 1914–1945.* Cambridge, Massachusetts: Harvard University Press, 2004.
U.S. Treasury Department. Foreign direct investment data. http://www.treas.gov/.
Organization for International Investment. "Insourcing Jobs by State." Fall 2007. http://www.ofii.org/docs/OFII_Job_Study.pdf.
Friedman, Thomas. *The World Is Flat.* New York: Farrar, Straus, and Giroux, 2005.

Chapter Two: The Invisible Worker

Howard, Brian. Interview by Mickey Meece, 2007.
King, Quentin. Interview by Mary M. Chapman, 2008.
Leonhardt, David. "$73 an Hour: Adding it Up," *New York Times,* December 9, 2008.
Obama, Barack. Campaign infomercial, October 29, 2008.
Whoriskey, Peter. "American Union Membership Grows After Bottoming Out." *Washington Post,* January 29, 2009.

Chapter Three: Foreign Capital

Mayerhuber, Wolfgang. Lufthansa news conference. December 14, 2007. TheStreet.com, http://www.thestreet.com/newsanalysis/transportation/10394649.html.
Sorkin, Andrew Ross. "Shift for Goldman and Morgan Marks the End of an Era." *New York Times,* September 21, 2008.
Vlasic, Bill. "Chrysler's New Ally Takes a Pragmatic Approach." *New York Times,* February 2, 2009.
Wikipedia, s.v. "News Corp." http://en.wikipedia.org/wiki/News_corp.
Wikipedia, s.v. "Sony." http://en.wikipedia.org/wiki/Sony.
Wilkins, Mira. *The History of Foreign Investment in the United States, 1914–1945.* Cambridge, Massachusetts: Harvard University Press, 2004.

Chapter Four: Not in My Backyard

"All Eyes on Whirlpool in Maytag Acquisition." Associated Press, July 20, 2005.

Dalal, Sucheta. "Mittal versus Arcelor: The Hypocrasy Within," *Indian Express*, March 6, 2006.

"Made in U.S.A.," *New Yorker*, March 16, 2009, p. 64.

"Recent Foreign Direct Manufacturing Investment in the United States." *Journal of International Business Studies* 1, no. 1 (Spring 2007).

Yi, Jeannie Jinsheng, and Shawn Xian Ye. *The Haier Way*. Dumont, New Jersey: Homa and Sekey Books, 2003.

Chapter Five: Not in Washington's Backyard, Either

Center for Responsible Politics. Toyota lobbying data. http://www.OpenSecrets.org.

CNN. *Lou Dobbs Tonight* transcript. May 9, 2005.

Foreign Affairs and International Trade Canada. "Softwood Lumber." http://www.international.gc.ca/controls-controles/softwood-bois_oeuvre/index.aspx?lang=eng.

Friedman, Thomas. "As Toyota Goes." *New York Times*, June 17, 2005.

———. "Et Tu, Toyota?" *New York Times*, October 3, 2007.

Gates, Dominic. "Huge Breaks for Aerospace." *Seattle Times*, December 17, 2007.

Powell, Stewart, M. "At Boeing, Shock, and Then Anger." *Seattle Post-Intelligencer*, February 29, 2008.

Shepardson, David. "Carmakers Ditch Scare Tactics in New Fuel Ads, *Detroit News*, July 14, 2007.

Talbot, George. "Shelby Rebukes Boeing in Letter." *Mobile Press-Register*, October 4, 2007.

"U.S. Lawmakers Blast Boeing Defense Contract Snub." Agence France-Presse, March 1, 2008.

Chapter Six: Foreign Owners, American Management

Bafunno, Norm, and Brian Howard. Interviews by Mickey Meece, 2007.

Haier headquarters. Notes from Kathryn Carlson, 2008.

Raskin, Andy. "When Your Customer Says Jump." *Business 2.0*, October 2003.

Yi, Jeannie Jinsheng, and Shawn Xian Ye. *The Haier Way*. Dumont, New Jersey: Homa and Sekey Books, 2003.

Chapter Seven: The Welcome Mat

Chapman, Mary M. "Piecemeal Recovery Fills a Void in a Former GM Town," *New York Times*, March 4, 2009.

Chapter Eight: The Race Between the States

Davey, Monica. "Economy Is Only Issue for Michigan Governor." *New York Times*, November 16, 2008.

Chapter Nine: View from the Top

Lippert, John, and Kae Inoue. "Toyota Recall Anxiety Accompanies Toyoda's Drive to President." Bloomberg News, July 24, 2007.

Chapter Ten: The New Face of the American Economy

CBS News. "Poll: American Split on Big 3 Bailout." December 8, 2008. http://www.cbsnews.com/stories/2008/12/08/opinion/polls/main4655829.shtml?source=RSS&attr=_4655829.

Fackler, Martin, and James Kanter. "Foreign Firms Linking Up for Piece of Stimulus." *New York Times*, February 5, 2009.

Friedman, Thomas. "The Open-Door Bailout." *New York Times*, February 11, 2009.

"The Return of Economic Nationalism." *Economist*, February 7, 2009.

Sanger, David. "Senate Agrees to Dilute 'Buy America' Provisions." *New York Times*, February 5, 2009.

Index

Abitibi-Consolidated, 126
Abu Dhabi, 36, 77
Adcock, Samuel, 23, 37, 116–117,
    119, 174
Aerospace AG, 110
Aerospatiale Matra, 110
Agnelli family, 81
Aguilera, Christina, 159
Aichi Forge USA, 164
Air France, 74
Airbus, 10, 11, 73, 109–110, 112,
    113, 246
Albright, Madeline, 247
Alcatel-Lucent, 238, 242
Alfa Romeo, 81
Alstom, 242
American Airlines, 74, 177
American Eurocopter, 48, 50–51,
    60, 111, 174, 177, 179–181, 187
American Exceptionalism, Myth of,
    30, 115
Anderson, Indiana, 168–171
Anheuser-Busch, 4, 35, 69, 71, 93,
    239
Arcelor, 90–91
ArcelorMittal, 35, 63, 91

Ardillo, Nick, 174, 177–180
Arista record label, 70
Astor, John Jacob, 19
Aurora Flight Sciences, 174

Bafunno, Norm, 139–143
Bain Capital, 102
Baker, Howard, 119
Banco de Bogotá, 71
Bancroft family, 70
Bank of America, 36
Bantam Books, 40, 70
Barbour, Haley Reeves, 125,
    186–194, 200, 207, 245
Barclays Capital, 36, 71, 239, 240
Barger, David, 74
Battle of the Overpass (1937),
    57–58
Bear Stearns, 75, 76
Bell Helicopter, 177
Bell Labs, 70, 238
Benoit, Jehane, 65
Berger, Sandy, 37
Bertelsmann, 39–40, 70
Bickson, Raymond, 96, 136–139
Blackstone Group, 36, 102

Blockade runners, 18–19
Blue Springs, Mississippi, 217, 245
BMW, 83
Boeing, 11, 29, 37, 40–41, 94,
    112–115, 245
Boeing, William E., 110
Borst, George, 101, 244
Branson, Richard, 93
Breton, Thierry, 91
Briem, Chris, 126–127
British Nobels, 68
Brownlee, Bruce, 107
Bruton, John, 235
Budget Rent A Car, 136
Buffalo, West Virginia, 34, 42
Bulcke, Paul, 168
Bush, George W., 102, 235
"Buy American" provision, 88–89,
    98, 230–231, 234–238

Cafeterias, 59
Call centers, 94
Campton Place Hotel, San
    Francisco, 92, 95
Camus, Philippe, 176
Carnegie, Andrew, 19
Casesa, John, 34, 123, 214
Caterpillar, 236
CBS Records, 71
Center for Responsive Politics, 120
Cerberus Capital Management,
    78–80
Chaison, Gary N., 25–26, 55, 64
Chapman, Marty, 26
Cheney, Dick, 19
Chevron, 102
China Investment Corporation, 77
China National Offshore Oil
    Corporation (CNOOC), 87,
    102–103

Cho, Fujio, 41, 141, 165–167,
    207–213, 224, 225
Chrysler Corporation, 35, 39, 56,
    63, 78–83, 94, 99, 123, 136, 143,
    194–196, 199, 209, 213, 229–
    230, 232–234, 240
Citigroup, 77
Civil War, 18–19, 24
Clinton, Bill, 37
Collins, Martha Layne, 164–165,
    167
Columbia Pictures, 71
Columbus, Mississippi, 48,
    171–175, 177–181
Construcciones Aeronauticas, 110
Continental Airlines, 74
Cooper, Jo, 37, 118–123
Cooper Tire & Rubber, 55
Corker, Bob, 232
Cost-of-living allowances, 61
Crosby, Ralph, 115, 116, 119
Cuneo, Dennis, 120, 165, 189,
    191–192, 197–198

Daimler-Benz, 79
DaimlerChrysler, 78, 79, 110, 176
Daniels, Mitch, 24, 169
Dearborn, Michigan, 57–58
Delta Air Lines, 30
Dingell, John, 37, 107–108
Dobbs, Lou, 117–118
Doubleday, 40, 70
Du Pont, Pierre S., 67–68
Dubai Ports World (DPW), 87–88
Durant, William C., 67

Eight O'Clock Coffee, 91–92, 97,
    131–133
Electrolux, 42
Embraer, 73

End of Detroit, The: How the Big Three Lost Their Grip on the American Car Market (Maynard), 195

Entitlement, sense of, 31

Estée Lauder, 1, 2, 7, 9

European Aeronautic Defence and Space Company (EADS), 3, 10–12, 29, 37, 40–41, 48, 87, 110–116, 119, 174–181, 187, 239, 245–247

Eurus Energy, 242

Farley, James, 136

Farnborough International Airshow, 109–110

Farnsworth, Bradley, 154

Fear, as reaction to foreign companies, 29–30, 87–88

Fearheiley, Robert C., 7

Federal Communications Commission (FCC), 117

Federal Reserve, 21

Ferree, Dan, 171

Fiat, 35, 39, 78–84, 135, 240

Financial crisis of 2008, 17, 21, 26, 42–43, 47, 62, 71, 75–76, 80, 100, 217, 229–231, 234, 236–243

Flynn, Judy, 49–51

Food Lion, 69

Ford, Henry, 57

Ford Motor Company, 20, 29, 39, 43, 56, 57, 67, 68, 79, 99, 124, 136, 194, 195, 199, 209–210, 213, 229–230, 233, 234

Fowles, Aaron S., 243

FOX Broadcasting Company, 70

Franco-German aircraft consortium, 3–4

Friedman, Thomas, 43, 121–122, 233, 237

GBL (global body line), 150

Geithner, Timothy, 230, 236, 237

General Accounting Office, 113

General Electric, 93, 101–102, 236

General Motors, 10, 20, 30, 43, 56, 63, 67–68, 79, 80, 89, 98, 99, 100, 120, 123, 124, 139–141, 151, 168–171, 194–196, 199, 209, 223, 229–230, 232–234, 244

Georgetown, Kentucky, 4–5, 27, 42, 52–53, 56, 61–62, 98, 144–146, 150, 161–167, 171, 179

Gettelfinger, Ron, 197

Ghosn, Carlos, 135

Gold mines, 19

Goldman Sachs, 76

Gone with the Wind (Mitchell), 19

Good, David, 95

Good Earth, 92, 133

Granholm, Jennifer Mulhern, 23, 107, 186–187, 194–200, 207

Great American Tea Company, 91–92

Great Atlantic and Pacific Company (A&P), 92, 132

Greensburg, Indiana, 54

Greenspan, Alan, 236–237

Grimes, Donald, 23, 30–31, 71, 89, 148, 247

Gross domestic product (GDP), 22, 42

Gryphon, 132, 133

Haier Group, 4, 10–12, 29, 41, 90, 93, 98, 101–103, 151–157, 204, 246, 247

Hailey, Clark, 115
Haines, Warren, 94
Harper, Bobby L., 172, 178
Harper, Stephen, 236
Health care benefits, 54, 59, 61, 62
Helú, Carlos Slim, 36, 240
Henderson, Fritz, 88–89
Hershey Company, 131
Hicks, Guy, 175
Hobson, David, 114
Hodges, Jim, 155
Honda, 3, 54, 81, 83, 98, 165, 169,
    171, 179, 188, 214, 233, 239
Horace, 227
Howard, Brian, 52–57, 61, 143–147
Howard, Stephanie, 52, 53
HSBC, 36
Hurricane Katrina, 126, 174, 187,
    190–192
Hyundai, 25, 62, 188, 193

Iacocca, Lee, 78, 93
IBAS (intelligent body assembly
    system), 149–151
Ibuka, Masaru, 70
InBev, 4, 35, 71, 93
INCAT, 94
Indian Hotels, 137–139
International Association of
    Machinists and Aerospace
    Workers, 32
International Steel Group, 63

Jaguar, 91, 92
Jamestown colony, 18
Jefferson, Thomas, 105
Jemal, Michael, 102, 103, 151,
    153–156
JetBlue Airways, 39, 72–75, 204
Job security, 8, 60

John Paul II, Pope, 183
Joint ventures, 38, 39, 63, 69
Juncker, Jean-Claude, 91

Kaizen, 140
Kamall, Syed, 235
Kant, Surya, 97
Kentucky, 4–5, 27, 41, 42, 52–53,
    54, 56, 61–62
Kia, 62, 188
King, Quentin, 63
Kirin Brewery, 76
KLM Royal Dutch Airlines, 74
Kraft Foods, 131
Krebs, Pam, 170
Kyl, John, 117

Labor, U.S. Department of, 60
Land Rover, 79, 91
Leaf Candy Company, 131
Lehman Brothers, 36, 71, 75, 76,
    239, 240
Lenovo, 89
Lever Brothers, 19
Lewis, John L., 45
Liess, James, 152
Liker, Jeffrey K., 98, 140–141
Lincoln, Abraham, 18
Lindsey, Amy, 1–2, 4–9, 142
Lost-day rates, 58
Lott, Trent, 37, 189, 197
Louisville Forge and Gear Works,
    164
Lufthansa, 39, 73–75, 84
Lutz, Robert, 120

Mack, John J., 77
Magel, Nick, 121
Marchionne, Sergio, 81–83, 135
Mark Hotel, New York, 137

Marx, Patricia, 89
Marysville, Ohio, 179
Mayrhuber, Wolfgang, 74–75
Maytag, 29, 90, 101–103
Mazda, 39, 98
McCain, John, 17, 113
McNerney, W. James, Jr., 114
Merced, Michael de la, 77–78
Mercedes-Benz, 3, 79, 83, 94, 165, 179, 188, 193, 239
Merrill Lynch, 36, 75
Metro-Goldwyn-Mayer (MGM), 71
Middlehoff, Thomas, 40
Mitsubishi car company, 39, 63, 76
Mitsubishi Group, 76
Mitsubishi UFJ Financial Group, 76–78, 84, 240
Mittal, Lakshmi, 90–91
Mobile, Alabama, 112
Morgan, Henry, 76
Morgan Stanley, 36, 75–78, 240
Morgenstern, Christian, 47
Mount Everest Mineral Water, 134
Murdoch, Rupert, 69

Nakanishi, Takaki, 216
Nano automobile, 29
Nardelli, Robert L., 80, 82
Nationalism, sense of, 31
Neeleman, David, 72, 73
Nestlé, 4, 42, 69, 168–171
New York Post, 69–70
New York Times, 61, 191, 233, 237, 238, 242
New York Times Company, 36, 240
New Yorker, 89
News Corporation, 69–70
Nikon, 76
Nissan, 3, 71, 79, 98, 135, 149, 151, 165, 188, 239

Nobel, Alfred, 68
Nobels Industries, 68
Nocera, Joe, 148, 157
Nokia, 42
North American Free Trade Agreement, 125–126
Northrop Grumman, 40, 112, 114, 115
NUMMI, 63, 223

Obama, Barack, 49, 56, 82, 88, 122, 123, 136, 186, 230, 234, 237, 238, 240–242
Off-shoring, 10
Ohno, Taiichi, 11, 208
Oil crisis of 1970s, 20, 124, 239
Oil prices, 73, 75, 194
Okamoto, Seizo, 141–142
Okuda, Hiroshi, 213
Olson, Lincoln, 114–115
Open Skies treaty, 74–75
Organization for International Investment (OFII), 25, 37–38, 69
Outsourcing, 10, 49, 94
Ownership stakes, 38, 39

PACCAR, 174
Paganini, Mark, 51, 111, 175–177, 180
Parking spaces, 59
Pelosi, Nancy, 113
Pierre Hotel, New York, 95, 138
Plant closings, 49, 50, 60
Polaroid, 117
Power, Peter, 235
Presidential election of 2008, 37, 49
Press, James, 136
Princeton, Indiana, 1–2, 139–143, 167, 217

Protectionism, 19–23, 25–26, 28–32, 38, 71, 87–91, 93–94, 98, 99, 100, 101, 109, 111, 114, 116, 124–127, 210, 230–231, 234–238, 240–242, 246, 247

Railroads, 19
Random House, 40, 70
Raskob, J. J., 68
Renault, 79, 135
Retirement plans, 54
Reuther, Walter, 58
Rhodes, James, 165
Rice, Condoleezza, 126
Riding, Alan, 133
Right to Work laws, 32, 54
Riley, Bob, 113
Ripplewood Holdings, 102
Ritz-Carlton Hotel, Boston, 95, 138
Rockefeller, Jay, 99, 226
Rosling, Alan, 90, 91, 94, 96, 97, 118, 127
Roth, Barbara, 97, 131–134
Ruimin, Zhang, 153, 156
Russell, Marty, 193
Ryan, Nevada, 47–49, 60

Safety rates, 58
San Antonio, Texas, 41, 61–62, 244–245
Sanyo, 242–243
Sephora, 69
September 2001 terrorist attacks, 73, 173
Severstal, 35, 174
Sharp, Isadore, 138
Shelby, Richard, 113
Sherman, Brad, 229–230
Siddhartha Gaitama (Buddha), 201

Slaughter, Matthew, 22
Smith, Kevin, 169
Smyrna, Tennesse, 149–150
Sony Corporation, 25, 70–71, 135, 149
Soros, George, 72
Southwest Airlines, 177, 204
Stabenow, Debbie, 198
Stanley, Harold, 76
Steel companies, 19, 35
Stengel, Casey, 129
Stringer, Howard, 135
Subaru, 169–170
Submarine cable network, 117–118
Sullenberger, Chesley, 11
Swoope, Gary, 181, 190–191, 193

Taj Hotel, Boston, 92, 95–96
Taj Hotel, Mumbai, 138–139
Target, 155
Tata, Ratan, 40, 93, 134, 137
Tata family, 135
Tata Group, 3, 10, 12, 29, 40, 41, 90–97, 92, 117–118, 132–134, 204, 246, 247
Tata Technologies, 94
Teamsters Union, 54
Tetley Tea, 92, 132
Tiahrt, Todd, 114
Toyoda, Akio, 41, 213, 217–226, 245
Toyoda, Kiichiro, 211, 213, 217, 224
Toyoda, Shoichiro, 213, 220, 223–225
Toyoda family, 135
Toyoda Machinery USA, 164
Toyota, 1–2, 4–10, 12, 26–29, 34, 39, 41, 53–55, 61–63, 71, 81, 97–100, 107–108, 118–123, 135,

136, 139–147, 149–151, 161–
    167, 169–171, 179, 187–194,
    196–198, 203–226, 233, 239,
    244–245, 247
Toyota Camry, 41
Toyota Prius, 121, 211, 212, 224,
    245
Toyota Production System (TPS),
    141–143, 208
Toyota Republicans, 232, 233
Toyota Sequoia, 139
Toyota Tundra, 41
Treasury, U.S. Department of, 21,
    22, 27, 32, 39, 43, 82, 117
Tupelo, Mississippi, 55, 164,
    189–194
Turner, Ted, 93
Twentieth Century Fox, 70
Tyco Global Network, 90, 96,
    117

UBS, 77
Unemployment rate, 22, 42, 195
Unilever, 19
Unions, 24, 32–33, 43, 50, 54–64,
    78, 82, 100, 171, 194, 197
United Airlines, 74
United Arab Emirates, 87
United Auto Workers (UAW), 32,
    43, 50, 54–58, 61, 63, 78, 82,
    171, 194, 197
United States Air Force, 4, 37, 40,
    110, 112–115, 172, 174,
    245–246
United States Army, 48
United Steelworkers, 32, 54
United Technologies, 49–50, 172
Universal Studios, 25
Unocal, 87, 102
UPS, 143

Vance, Alabama, 179
Virgin Atlantic, 93
Virginia Company, 18
Visclosky, Pete, 234
Volkswagen, 42, 81
Volvo, 79
VSNL (Videsh Sanchar Nigam
    Limited), 117–118

Wage rates, 32, 54, 61–62
Wagoner, Rick, 123
Walmart, 22, 155
Watanabe, Katsuaki, 190, 193,
    212–217, 219, 223–225
Welbilt, 153
Welch, Jack, 93
Wellspring, Mississippi, 191–192
Wellstone, Paul, 15
Wenders, Wim, 85
Weyerhaeuser, 126
Whirlpool Corporation, 29, 102,
    103
Wilkins, Mira, 125
Williamstown, Kentucky, 52
Windham Hill Records, 70
Womack, James P., 208, 222
World Is Flat, The (Friedman), 43,
    181
World Trade Organization, 125
World War I, 19, 67
World War II, 20, 67

Xenophobia, 89, 98, 162

Yokoi, Hirofumi, 213
York Township, Michigan, 28, 107

Zinn, Howard, 30

ABOUT THE AUTHOR

MICHELINE MAYNARD joined the *New York Times* staff in 2004 as a reporter in Business Day, covering the airline industry. Known as Micki, she was named Detroit bureau chief in October 2005, where she directed the *Times*' reporting of the automobile industry. She became a senior business correspondent in 2008, covering transportation issues. She also contributes to the Dining and Travel sections.

In 2009, she was named the eleventh winner of the annual Nathaniel Nash Award, which honors a *Times* reporter who excels in business and economics coverage, at home or abroad. She has won the paper's Publisher's Award five times.

She has written for *Fortune* magazine and been a staff writer or bureau chief at news organizations, including *USA Today*, *Newsday*, *U.S. News & World Report*, and the Reuters News Service. She began her career as a legislative correspondent for United Press International in Lansing, Michigan, and served as an intern in the White House Press Office.

Micki is an adjunct faculty member at the Ross School of Business at the University of Michigan and has taught at the Wharton School at the University of Pennsylvania.

She was named a media fellow by the Japan Society of New York in 2002 and also was a Knight-Wallace Fellow at the University of Michigan in 1999 through 2000. In 1989 through 1990, she was chosen as a Knight-Bagehot Fellow in business and economics journalism at Columbia University. She holds an undergraduate degree from Michigan State University and a graduate degree from Columbia University.

She is the author of four books, including *The End of Detroit: How the Big Three Lost Their Grip on the American Car Market*, which was published in hardcover by Doubleday in 2003 and in paperback in 2004.